the quick grill

artist

fast and fabulous recipes

for cooking with fire

norman kolpas

photographs by brian leatart

Clarkson Potter/Publishers
New York

Published by Clarkson Potter/Publishers, New York, New York.
Member of the Crown Publishing Group, a division of Random House, Inc.
www.randomhouse.com

CLARKSON N. POTTER is a trademark and POTTER and colophon are registered trademarks of
Random House, Inc.

Printed in the United States of America

Design by Jan Derevjanik

Library of Congress Cataloging-in-Publication Data
Kolpas, Norman.
    The quick grill artist : fast and fabulous recipes for cooking with fire / Norman Kolpas.
        p.   cm.
    Includes index.
    1. Barbecue cookery.   2. Quick and easy cookery.   I. Title.
TX840.B3 K65   2002
641.5'74—dc21   2001036756

ISBN 0-609-60951-3

10   9   8   7   6   5   4   3   2   1

First Edition

acknowledgments

First thanks go to my agent and friend, Nancy Crossman. She understood this project from the start, and her creativity, editorial and publishing savvy, and good cheer contributed enormously to its successful completion.

Katie Workman at Clarkson Potter tuned in to the book right away. I've greatly appreciated her intelligent enthusiasm for it. Katherine Flanagan-Hyde and Elaina Lin at Potter kept communications flowing with great courtesy and efficiency. Photographer Brian Leatart, food stylist Valerie Aikman-Smith, and their team really helped the recipes come alive. Thanks also to Jan Derevjanik, Sibylle Kazeroid, and Alison Forner.

Many people participated in the book's creation throughout the months of recipe-testing sessions: Brendan "Ronaldo" Bigelow, Evan Bigelow, Michele Bigelow, Jack Eller, Mary Eller, Dr. Hubert Goldman, Alexander Kalman, Mary Kalman, Vanessa Kramer, Linda Peterson, Adam Rosenstein, Eric Rosenstein, Michael Rubin, Susan Rubin, Chuck Stewart, and Carol Zeitz. Thank you all.

My two most devoted testers, however, deserve the greatest thanks: my wife, Katie, and our son, Jake. They both submitted themselves happily to what sometimes seemed like an endless procession of meals cooked on our patio. Katie unwaveringly volunteered to do the cleanup chores, as well as provided some smart ideas for things she might especially like to eat. Jake was a constant source of ideas and suggestions for recipes. This book is lovingly dedicated to them both.

contents

intro
duction

When I get the urge to grill I want good, delicious, creative, easy-to-make food—and I want it *now*. I don't want to go on a shopping scavenger hunt. I don't want to plunge into elaborate advance preparations—or to have to plan ahead at all. I don't want to wait for my main ingredients to marinate several hours or overnight. I don't want to have to do much additional cooking away from the grill, if any. And once I've got the food on the fire, I don't want to have to wait any more than half an hour, at the *very* most, to eat it.

That's what *The Quick Grill Artist* is all about: instant gratification of the best sort. All the recipes in this book have been devised with a few simple goals in mind:

*   **They're fast and easy to prepare.** They can be readied for cooking, start to finish, in a matter of minutes at the least—and at most in no more time than it takes to heat up the fire in an outdoor grill.

*   **They cook quickly.** Once they're on the grill, most recipes cook in less than 15 minutes, and all in less than 30.

*   **The results are creative and delicious.** Minimal effort yields maximum flavor, allowing you easily to make a great impression whether you're serving family or friends, at a casual cookout or a special occasion.

*   **The ingredients are easy to find.** You can buy everything in most well-stocked supermarkets (though an ethnic market or gourmet store may occasionally make your quest easier).

*   **The equipment is simple.** These recipes don't require that you have any specialized equipment beyond a decent outdoor (or indoor) grill and basic, good-quality grilling utensils.

In short, this book aims to turn you into a Quick Grill Artist. And you don't have to spend even a moment in art—or grilling—school to become one.

how to become
a quick grill artist

The following few key principles will turn anyone into a Quick Grill Artist. You can master these virtually in the time it takes to read them, and you'll be able to apply the basic techniques to other dishes you might well be inspired to create yourself.

* **Use quality ingredients.** Nothing affects the final results of your cooking more than the quality of the ingredients you begin with. Make yourself an informed shopper. Check out your local newspaper food section, food magazines, and ingredient reference books, and ask questions of your family members, friends, acquaintances, and market personnel. You'll begin to learn how to spot the best ingredients and where to buy them in your area. Common sense, combined with well-attuned senses, are your best allies. Your eyes, hands, and nose will tell you if something is in peak quality or not. Don't settle for second best.

* **Pick fast-cooking cuts.** Quick grilling rules out large cuts of meat and big, whole fish or whole poultry slowly turning on a rotisserie suspended over the fire. Those cuts all take way too long to cook, and require you to build and sometimes replenish an indirect-heat fire. For the 30 minutes or less of cooking time that quick grilling requires, opt for steaks, chops, slender tenderloins, boneless and skinless chicken pieces, and seafood fillets.

* **Select intense flavors.** Long, slow marinating that saturates food with flavor can take hours. Quick grilling instead relies on seasoning food with intense or concentrated flavors—chili peppers, garlic, herbs, spices, mustards, oils, pickles, preserves—that deliver a maximum flavor impact in minimal time.

* **Pound it.** A number of the recipes in this book benefit from a brief pounding on the kitchen counter with a heavy, specially designed meat pounder or mallet (available in kitchen equipment stores) or a solid, heavy wooden rolling pin. This flattens meat or poultry cuts so they'll cook more quickly and evenly. In the process, it breaks down their muscle fibers, yielding even greater tenderness while also enabling seasonings to penetrate more quickly.

* **Rub or smear on flavor.** Seasoning blends that you rub on dry, or mix with a little oil or another liquid to form a paste, have become very popular in recent years. You'll find prepared blends in the seasonings aisle of your market as well as in the

meat and seafood departments, in specialty cookware stores, and in shops or even hardware stores devoted to grills and grilling equipment. But it's more fun and creative to make rubs and pastes yourself. A number of the recipes in this book—including Cowboy Steaks with Redeye Chili Rub (page 49), Jamaican-Style Jerked Pork Tenderloin (page 72), Spicy Buttermilk Chicken Breasts (page 89), Four-Flavor Popcorn Shrimp (page 111), Moroccan Swordfish Kebabs (page 123), and Miso-Ginger Eggplant (page 134)—owe their great taste to just such simple seasoning blends.

* **Marinate briefly.** When other grilling books call for foods to be marinated, doing so can take hours. But quick-cooking cuts of meat, poultry, and seafood can benefit from even brief marinating, especially when intense flavorings are used and when denser-textured meat or poultry is first pounded, as in the recipes for Cuban Steaks with Garlic-Citrus Marinade and Orange-Onion Salsa (page 52), Mongolian Lamb (page 84), and Spanish-Style Garlic Shrimp Skewers (page 108).

* **Brush on flavor.** Basting with a marinade or sauce adds flavor right on the grill, as well as keeps food moist. You'll find various flavorful bastes used throughout this book. Some are marinades in which the food also briefly soaks, as in the recipes for Chipotle-Orange Veal Chops (page 64) and Mint-Soy Lamb Chops (page 76). (I favor dividing such mixtures into two batches, one for marinating, one for basting, to avoid the risk of bacterial contamination.) And some are glazes, which coat the food with a glossy, flavorful sheen during the final minutes of cooking. Examples include Pork Chops with Maple-Cider Glaze (page 66), Caribbean Chicken Thighs with Molasses, Black Pepper, and Orange Glaze (page 99), Soy- and Honey-Glazed Scallop Skewers (page 112), and Balsamic-Glazed Red Onions (page 139).

* **Inject flavor.** A few of the recipes for larger cuts of meat, including Self-Basting Garlic-Pepper Steak (page 59) and Three-Chili-Glazed Pork Tenderloin (page 68), call for liquid seasoning mixtures to be injected, which both seasons the meat and bastes it from the inside out. You can accomplish this with a meat syringe composed of a large hypodermic-like chamber with plunger and a sturdy, long, screw-on needle with a big hole or two at the end. Such devices can be found in well-stocked kitchen supply stores. You don't need to run out and search for one now; but if the idea appeals to you, or you come across one of these syringes, the results are surprising and delightful.

* **Blend in flavor.** Grilling ground meat, poultry, or seafood gives you an excellent opportunity to incorporate seasonings. Several recipes in this book—including Pizzaiola Burgers (page 62), Middle Eastern Minced Lamb Kebabs with Tzatziki and

Mint-Onion Relish (page 82), Thanksgiving Turkey Burgers with Sage, Onion, and Cranberry Sauce (page 106), and Salmon Burgers Teriyaki with Japanese Cucumbers and Wasabi-Dijon Mustard (page 118)—gain substantial flavor, not to mention added succulence, from other ingredients blended into the ground mixtures.

* **Stuff it.** A simple stuffing of cheese, ham, herbs, or other flavorful embellishments artistically enhances grilled recipes with just a little extra effort. One of the easiest ways to stuff foods for grilling is to pound them flat and fold them around the other ingredients, securing the edges with large wooden cocktail toothpicks to form a neat package. You'll find this technique used in Veal Pockets with Smoked Mozzarella and Anchovy (page 65) and Chicken Breasts Stuffed with Provolone, Ham, and Sage (page 94).

* **Stack it.** Even easier than stuffing is stacking: topping grilled foods during the final minutes of cooking with small, intensely flavored ingredients that will heat through quickly, as in the recipes for Chicken Breasts Napolitano (page 86) and Tricolore Tomato Stacks (page 130). Cheese is usually the topmost layer in such stacks, melting to seal in the other ingredients.

* **Wrap it.** An edible wrapper makes an impressive embellishment for grilled foods, adding flavor, holding in other seasonings, and helping to keep the foods within moist. The most common form of edible wrapper is usually ham or bacon, used in such recipes as Bacon-Wrapped Cheddar Dogs (page 74), Prosciutto-Wrapped Lemon-Basil Scallops (page 113), and Bacon-Wrapped Brandied Dried Plums (page 166). Another attractive, unusual, and delicious wrapper is grape leaves, which appear in Feta Cheese Wrapped in Grape Leaves (page 46) and Lemon-and-Dill-Scented Trout in Grape Leaves (page 128).

* **Make a simple sauce.** There are times when you have such beautiful main ingredients—a prime steak, a meaty chop, a perfectly trimmed chicken breast, an exquisite fresh fish fillet—that you don't want to tinker with perfection. That's the time for the Quick Grill Artist to prepare a simple sauce to complement the main dish at serving time. Some of the easiest of all such sauces are seasoned butters. They are featured in such recipes as Steaks with Chipotle-Garlic Chili Butter (page 56), Chicken Breasts with Sesame-Soy-Ginger Butter (page 88), Turkey Breast Cutlets with Pesto Butter (page 102), Swordfish with Anchovy-Lemon Butter (page 124), and Portobello Mushrooms with Garlic-Parsley-Basil Butter (page 151). Even more impressive is a chunky, fresh salsa or relish that offers complementary and contrasting colors,

tastes, and textures. Good examples include Greek Lamb Chops with Feta and Kalamata Olive Salsa (page 78), Tandoori-Style Leg of Lamb with Vegetable-Herb Raita (page 80), Tuna Provençale (page 120), and Blackened Red Snapper with Quick Tropical Salsa (page 126).

* **Add a grilled accompaniment.** Often the dishes you serve along with your main course can make an eloquent artistic statement. That's why this book offers a wealth of grilled vegetable dishes (pages 129–162) as well as breads and toasts (pages 27–47) that are easily cooked at the same time that the main dish is on the grill. Sometimes accompaniments become part of the dish itself, as they do in Springtime Chicken Tender and Baby Artichoke Kebabs (page 96) or Sea Bass and Mushroom Kebabs with Ginger and Scallions (page 125).

* **Cross-hatch it.** Many grilled dishes in restaurants look so impressive because they're artfully cross-hatched with marks from the bars of the grill rack. With hardly any extra effort, you can achieve the same effect with the recipes in this book. All you have to do is rotate the position of a piece of food on the grill rack by 90 degrees on each side (the equivalent of 3 hours on a clock dial) halfway through its cooking time.

* **Present it artfully.** Your final, and sometimes best, opportunity for Quick Grill Artistry comes when you move the finished food from the grill to a serving platter or individual serving plate. You can make a big impression simply by serving your food on your best dinnerware instead of on plastic or paper plates. Give a moment's thought to how you position the food on the platter or plate for the best eye appeal. A platter of food, for example, can look more attractive when individual servings such as steaks, chops, or fish fillets are positioned so they partially overlap. Many of the recipes suggest garnishes of herbs or lemon wedges, which add contrasts of shape and color. Accompanying sauces or salsas may be pooled on the plate before the food is attractively placed on top, or appealingly heaped on top or just to the side of the food.

a quick guide to picking the right grill

If you have this book in your hands, you probably already own a grill. So it would be pointless, if not downright rude, to tell you that one type of grill is better than another for the Quick Grill Artist.

Fortunately, you can make the recipes in this book with virtually any kind of grill. But the size of your outdoor grill's cooking surface (and, to a lesser extent, that of certain indoor grills) may limit the types or quantities of certain foods you can prepare at one time (see "Charcoal Grills," below).

Other grilling books give much more extensive and strict guidance on choosing a grill—and for a good reason: More time-consuming or elaborate recipes require equipment that can keep a fire going longer, spin a roast on a rotisserie, or perform other complicated feats that are of no concern for a Quick Grill Artist.

gas grills

A refillable propane tank or a natural gas line provides the fuel for these grills, heating a permanent bed of lava rocks or ceramic briquettes beneath the grill rack. Gas grills offer the advantages of quick and easy fire starting and simple cleanup. They are used outdoors in most cases but may also be found built in to some upscale kitchens with special ventilation for their heat and smoke. (Do not move any grill intended for outdoor use into your home.) These grills tend to be on the larger side, so virtually any will work well for the recipes in this book. (Those with separate controls for burners under two halves of the fire bed offer you greater flexibility while grilling, which is necessary for the grilled pizza recipes on pages 41–45.)

charcoal grills

These work fine for quick grilling. The smallest, cast-iron, Japanese-style hibachis will limit the quantity of food you can cook at one time, however, restricting you from cooking larger items or multiple quantities or recipes. Flat-bottomed, brazier-type, larger kettle-style grills or built-in brick charcoal grills will all generally provide ample cooking surfaces for one or more recipes.

indoor electric grills

These items fall into two categories. The most basic indoor grills feature an electric heating element beneath a grill rack; they may be countertop models or built in to some stoves, and will work well for all recipes, provided they offer an adequately sized cooking surface.

Also popular nowadays are the two-sided, hinged electric countertop grills that have solid, ridged, heated surfaces; the best known of these grills bear the name of a famous heavyweight boxing champion. The size of their cooking surfaces will limit the amount and size of the foods you can cook on them. They'll work best for recipes featuring ingredients with flat surfaces of a uniform thickness no greater than about 1 inch—and with ingredients not placed on skewers, as some skewers may interfere with the closing of the hinged top grill plate. When cooking any recipe in this book on such a grill, note that since it cooks from both sides simultaneously, the total cooking time called for will be halved.

grill pans

Made of cast iron or heavy-grade aluminum, these solid ridged pans, heated on a burner on your stove, actually more closely approximate pan-frying or griddling in the way they cook than they do grilling. Nevertheless, the searing action of their raised ridges, and the marks the ridges leave on food, simulate the effect of grilling. Depending on their size, grill pans will work well for the recipes in this book. Make sure, however, that you use them with good ventilation to whisk away the smoke and heat.

a quick guide to fuels and fire-building

Quick grilling relies on your having a good, reliable, easy-to-use source of fuel readily at hand whenever you want to grill.

for gas grills

Gas grills are fueled by either natural gas or propane.

natural gas ✻ My grilling life has never been simpler since I had my gas grill hooked up to a natural gas line on my patio. All I have to do when I want to grill is turn the line's valve lever to the On position, then start up the grill. The natural gas gives me a steady, clean, reliable source of fuel.

I was fortunate, of course, that our home was built with that gas line already in place—and even more fortunate that when the hookup was attempted for the first time about 20 years after our home was built, the line was in perfect working order.

If your own home has such a working outdoor line, I heartily recommend that you use it for a gas grill. Note that natural gas requires an adaptation to the grill's burner elements for the fire to burn properly. Make sure that a professional installer does the adaptation for you.

I also strongly urge you to have the hookup done by a professional: either the installation specialist from the store where you bought the grill or someone from your local utilities company. Likewise, if you want to put a gas line in, have the work done by an expert.

propane * Propane, sold in refillable tanks at grill specialty stores and hardware stores, is also an outstanding fuel source for gas grills. It's a good idea to check the gauge on your propane tank (after turning the tank to the On position) to ensure that you have sufficient fuel for grilling. In addition, you should have a spare full tank on hand. A standard propane tank should keep your grill going for 12 to 18 hours. Always diligently follow the hookup instructions and precautions printed on your propane tank.

starting a gas grill fire

The shortest answer on how to start a fire in a gas grill is to read your grill's instructions: each make and model will have its own specific guidelines for a safe, efficient start. In general, however, starting such a grill will involve turning on the gas source and then lighting the burners. More expensive grill models will include a built-in sparking device to ignite the gas. Otherwise, use long fireplace matches for safe starting. A gas grill needs starting at least 15 minutes in advance to heat up its bed of lava rocks or ceramic briquettes before it is ready for cooking chores.

for charcoal grills

A number of different fuel options are available for charcoal grills.

lump charcoal * Made by burning aged hardwood in a kiln, this form of charcoal is hard to find and more expensive than other choices, and can throw off sparks.

But it yields a clean, hot fire and adds a hint of scent from the wood—usually mesquite or hickory—from which it was made.

hardwood charcoal briquettes * These are made by compacting powdered lump charcoal with natural binders into compact, even, uniform pillow-shaped briquettes. They are easier to find than lump charcoal and provide a good, hot fire.

composition briquettes * Other binders and fillers may be added to these, the most common type of barbecue briquettes and also the cheapest. The best brands will work fine.

self-lighting briquettes * Some fuels are just too quick. These briquettes, presaturated with petroleum-based lighter fluid, can give an off flavor to grilled foods.

starting a charcoal grill fire

First, fill the fire bed of your grill with enough charcoal to form a uniform layer when spread evenly over the bottom of the grate. Then, start the fire in one of the following recommended ways.

chimney starter * These wide metal cylinders are sold in grill shops and hardware stores, as well as in some markets that carry fuels. Place a chimney starter on the grill's fire bed and pile the charcoal inside atop its built-in grate. Stuff crumpled newspapers in the area below the chimney's grate and light them with wooden matches. In about 20 minutes, the coals should be uniformly covered with white ash, an indication that they're ready to be dumped out into the grill bed and spread out for cooking.

pyramid method * Gather your unlit charcoal into a pyramid-shaped mound, a compact form that will concentrate and conserve heat so the coals reach cooking temperature in the minimum amount of time. A pyramid can be lit in a number of ways: with an electric fire-starting coil, atop which the pyramid is built; with easy-to-light, commercially sold paraffin-soaked corncobs or sticks that you include inside the base of the pyramid; or with an alcohol-based commercial fire-starting gel squirted onto the coals themselves and then lit with a match. (Do not use old-fashioned liquid lighter fluids, which can pollute and are now banned in some areas.) A pyramid of coals will be covered in white ash and ready to spread and use in 20 to 30 minutes.

a quick guide to grilling tools and accessories

A Quick Grill Artist doesn't get burdened with too many gadgets for the grill. Use the following as your guide.

*   **Long-handled utensils.** Long handles let you move foods on the fire with less risk of exposing your hands or arms to intense heat. Most useful are a wide metal spatula for flipping burgers and fish fillets, and tongs for turning more awkwardly shaped or larger items, from kebabs to chicken pieces to big steaks. A two-pronged fork is also good for spearing and turning large items. It can be even more useful if it includes a built-in doneness gauge (see "Cooking Times and Tests for Doneness," page 21). Keep an extra pair of heatproof long-handled tongs next to a charcoal grill for spreading out just-lit coals into an even bed.

*   **Grill brush.** A brush with stiff metal bristles, a metal scraping plate, and a long handle will help you scrape food residue from the grill rack just before or after cooking.

*   **Basting brush.** Use a long-handled brush with soft natural bristles to baste foods with marinades, sauces, and glazes. You can also use this to brush the grill rack with oil before cooking.

*   **Grilling glove.** Resembling an oven mitt, this fireproof glove offers added protection to the hand wielding the tools during grilling.

*   **Instant-read thermometer.** A pocket-sized instant-read thermometer will quickly register internal temperatures when inserted into the thickest part of a piece of food on the grill, and it provides a fast, handy way to gauge doneness. Some special grilling forks now include such gauges built in to their handles.

*   **Skewers.** These sharp-tipped little spears hold together smaller pieces of food on the grill. The simplest are wooden or bamboo skewers, which should be soaked in cold water for at least 15 minutes before use to help keep them from charring during grilling. Better still, buy a set of metal skewers. Look for those with flattened blades that will hold foods more securely, preventing them from spinning or falling off. And avoid those with bulky decorative handles that might prevent kebabs from sitting evenly or turning easily on the grill.

* **Grill baskets and small-meshed grill screens.** The recipes in this book all aim to eliminate the need for such specialized paraphernalia. If you have one of these, though, it can at times give you an extra sense of security when grilling delicate fish or small pieces of food that run the risk of falling through an ordinary grill rack.

* **Flashlight or grill light.** Some Quick Grill Artists don't let the time of day or time of year stop them from grilling. If you're ever likely to cook outdoors after dark, a handheld flashlight or a special clip-on light can help you better see what's happening on the grill.

quick grilling techniques and strategies

You'll find all the instructions you need for grilling efficiently in each of the recipes in this book. Nonetheless, it's a good idea to review the basics of quick grilling.

the direct-heat method

Almost every recipe in this book cooks by direct heat—that is, by placing and cooking the food on the grill rack directly over the heat. That requires you simply to heat a gas grill or spread a bed of heated charcoals directly under the area of the grill rack on which you'll be cooking. One notable exception, however, is grilled pizza (pages 41–45). Pizza cooks best on a hot grill rack set off away from the fire. If you plan to start a meal with grilled pizza, spread the hot coals (or light the gas element) in just one half of the grill's fire bed, then cook the pizza as described on the grill rack above the other half of the fire bed.

getting ready to cook

To help any recipe proceed more quickly and efficiently, read it over thoroughly. Just before you're about to cook, bring all foods that will be grilled (including any bastes, garnishes, tools, or other items you'll need), out to the grill. Array them on the grill's built-in tray or on a convenient tray or table near the grill.

oiling the grill rack

All the recipes in this book call for the grill rack to be oiled before the food is placed upon it—a simple step that helps prevent food from sticking. Use a flavorless cooking oil, or the same type of flavored oil called for in the recipe, pouring about 2 tablespoons in a small bowl. A long-handled basting brush may be used to brush the oil onto the grill rack. Or follow the practice of some Japanese cooks: Fold a clean but worn-out kitchen towel in half lengthwise, then roll it up tightly and tie it securely in two or three places with kitchen string. Dip one end into the oil and then swab it over the grill rack.

covering the grill

A few recipes in this book call for the grill to be covered briefly during cooking. Most grills today have built-in covers. If yours does not, consider buying a large domed wok lid with a heatproof handle from a kitchen supply store. Place the lid over the food directly on the grill when necessary.

cooking times and tests for doneness

I've never met a grilling time chart I fully trust. That, in brief, is why you won't find the usual time charts in this book telling you how long to grill a particular cut or thickness of meat for rare, medium-rare, or medium, or how many minutes chicken breasts or fish fillets need to cook through.

Why aren't grilling charts entirely reliable? The answer is that so many different factors contribute to how long something takes to cook: the particular kind of equipment you use, the type of fuel, the size and thickness of your main ingredients, the effect of other ingredients in the recipe, the temperature of the food when it hits the grill, the outdoor (or indoor) temperature at the time you're cooking, and even whether or not there's a breeze (and possibly, though I've never tested for it, the alignment of the planets and stars at that particular moment of cooking). Not to mention how you personally might define rare or medium-rare or medium.

As a result, no matter what chart I consult, sooner rather than later I find that something I've cooked on my grill is done to my liking before or after the given time range. So invariably, I toss the chart aside and trust my own judgment.

I'd like you to gain the confidence and the insight to do the same.

For each recipe in this book, I give an approximate cooking time or time range based on my testing of that particular recipe. Use that given time as only a rough guide to your own cooking time on your grill.

More important, use your senses. Train yourself to look for the signs that indicate when something is cooked through or done to your liking.

Often, looking simply involves cutting a sample serving of meat or chicken (invariably yours, as the cook) to see what it's like inside. Or stick an instant-read thermometer or a thermometer/fork into the center of a large cut of meat to gauge its internal temperature.

meat

To test for doneness, cut into the thickest part of a sample piece of meat at the earliest possible time given in the recipe. Rare meat will look a deep rose color in the center, medium-rare will be light pink, and medium will have just a hint of pinkness left in the center. Cook all burgers at least to medium or medium-well to kill off any possible bacteria. Pork should be cooked medium to medium-well also. Corresponding temperatures from an instant-read thermometer are 120° to 125°F for rare, 130°F for medium-rare, and 140°F for medium. Cook pork to 150° to 160°F.

poultry

No trace of pink should remain when the thickest part of a piece of grilled poultry is cut into. On an instant-read thermometer, white meat should register 165° to 170°F, dark meat 180°F.

seafood

When the tip of a small, sharp knife is inserted into the thickest part of a piece of fish, it should appear firm and flaky but still moist. One exception is ahi tuna, which is popular nowadays cooked rare to medium-rare. Like steaks, ahi tuna cooked this way will be rosy pink to lightly pink at the center.

grill cleanup and maintenance

A Quick Grill Artist knows that a little bit of cleanup after cooking will help avoid time-consuming work the next time you decide to grill. Review the instructions for your grill brand and model for specific cleaning guidelines.

cleaning the grill rack

After cooking, leave the grill rack over the hot fire for 10 to 15 minutes. Then, with the rack still over the fire, give it a good scrubbing using the bristles and, if necessary, the scraping blade of a metal-bristled grill brush. In most cases, this will effectively clean the grill rack. After a brief brushing, it will be ready to use the next time you grill.

cleaning the lid

While the grill is still warm but not hot, use paper towels to wipe away any grease from inside the lid.

cleaning the exterior

Periodically clean off your grill's exterior with warm, soapy water and a cloth, then rinse well and wipe dry with a clean cloth.

cleaning out a gas grill

After the fire bed of a gas grill has cooled completely, remove any particles of food or other residue that has fallen into the lava rock or ceramic briquette fire bed. Periodically clean out the tubes leading to the burners (venturi tubes is the technical term), following your owner's manual. You can also have a professional from a grill store service the grill for you, checking for any leaks or kinks in the valves or lines.

cleaning out a charcoal grill

Several hours after cooking—or the next day, after the fire has died away completely with no trace of heat or live embers—dispose of the ashes in a responsible way. Use a metal shovel to transfer them to a trash receptacle. You may also spread the ashes in your garden beds if they are suitable for the plants you're growing.

a guide to quick grilling safety

Never let quickness or artistry get in the way of safety when you grill. At all times, let common sense be your guide to ensure that the food you cook and eat, the equipment you use, and your grill's surroundings do not become hazardous to you, your guests, your family, or your home.

* Grill only in a well-ventilated area, clear of any structures, overhangs, plants, or other flammable or combustible objects and materials.

* Keep small children and animals safely away from the grill at all times.

* Make sure that your grill is in good, safe working order before starting a fire.

* Store fuels and fire-starting materials responsibly and safely.

* Avoid wearing loose-fitting clothing that could catch fire. Roll up your sleeves before starting the fire or cooking on the grill.

* If you use an electric fire starter, keep its cord clear of the fire and of possible tripping hazards. After use, let the starter cool down completely in a safe, fireproof place before storing it.

* If you use frozen meat, poultry, or seafood, thaw it in the refrigerator or microwave oven—never out in the open at room temperature.

* Always use clean hands when you handle food. After handling raw meat, poultry, or seafood, wash your hands with lots of warm, soapy water, rinse well, and dry with a clean towel.

* Always use clean utensils, dishes, cutting boards, and other equipment to avoid cross-contamination by food-borne bacteria, especially from raw meat, poultry, and seafood.

* Do not leave uncooked foods out at room temperature or in the open air for long periods of time. This can promote bacterial growth. However, foods can be taken from the refrigerator and left safely at room temperature for the relatively brief time it takes to prepare them while the grill is heating. If you prep the foods further in advance, cover and refrigerate them until you're ready to cook them.

* To prevent the possibility of bacterial growth, cover and refrigerate leftovers soon after eating.

appetizers, breads, & pizzas

Take a bite of a great appetizer, and you just know that the rest of the meal is likely to be terrific. When that appetizer comes hot off the grill, the impression it makes is doubly dazzling.

Bread-based appetizers, from seasoned toasts to quesadillas to true grilled sandwiches, have a featured role in this chapter because they're so swiftly prepared and toasted in minutes on the grill. They make an appealing snack in their own right or a fitting accompaniment either to another appetizer or to a hot-off-the-grill main course. Some of the most stunning such appetizers are grilled pizzas, pages 41–45, an easy-to-master specialty that will draw raves from your guests.

The appeal of cheese melted above a live fire also translates into two other dishes that conclude the chapter: Grilled Camembert Salad, a simple salad topped with wedges cut from whole grilled camembert (page 47), and Feta Cheese Wrapped in Grape Leaves, fingers of tangy feta cheese shielded and contained by edible grape-leaf wrappers (page 46). Bear in mind that many of the vegetable recipes in this book (pages 129–162), as well as the shrimp and scallop recipes (pages 108–113), can also quickly and artistically start a meal.

two-cheese quesadillas

This is the quesadilla at its simplest, brushed with aromatic olive oil and filled with two favorite complementary Southwestern cheeses.

—— 4 servings ——

4 **large flour tortillas**

¼ **cup extra-virgin olive oil**

¼ **pound Monterey Jack cheese, shredded**

¼ **pound sharp Cheddar cheese, shredded**

Preheat the grill.

Carefully oil the grill rack. Brush one side of each tortilla evenly with the olive oil, then place the tortillas oiled side down on the grill. Immediately spread the shredded cheese evenly on top of half of each tortilla. With tongs, fold the uncovered half of the tortilla over the cheese. Cook until the cheese has melted and the tortillas are golden brown on both sides, turning once, 3 to 4 minutes total cooking time.

With the tongs or a spatula, remove the quesadillas from the grill. Transfer the quesadillas to a cutting board and, with a sharp knife, cut into wedges.

quicktips & variations

* Buy preshredded cheeses to save yourself time in the kitchen.
* Vary the cheese mixture to your tastes. Try some crumbled white Mexican cheese such as *cotija*.
* Add a light sprinkling of herbs when you spread the cheeses on the tortillas. Crumbled dried oregano or finely chopped fresh cilantro are good choices.

quesadillas
with goat cheese and damson jam

Rich, tangy goat cheese and tart-sweet plum jam form a sophisticated partnership in this unusual, delicious appetizer for a special grill party. It's a particularly fitting starter for a meal featuring grilled lamb.

— 4 servings —

Preheat the grill.

Just before cooking, brush one side of each tortilla with the melted butter. Carefully oil the grill rack and place the tortillas buttered side down on the rack. With a long-handled knife, spatula, or the back of a long-handled spoon, immediately spread the jam over the entire top of each tortilla and then quickly distribute the goat cheese over half of the surface. With tongs, immediately fold the other half of the tortilla over the cheese. Cook until the cheese has melted and the tortillas are golden brown on both sides, turning once, 3 to 4 minutes total cooking time.

With the tongs or a spatula, remove the quesadillas from the grill. Transfer the quesadillas to a cutting board and, with a sharp knife, cut into wedges.

4 large flour tortillas

4 tablespoons unsalted butter, melted

8 tablespoons damson jam

8 ounces fresh, creamy goat cheese, crumbled or cut into thin disks

quick tips & variations

* Once a rare import from France, fresh goat cheese is now widely made domestically and can be found in well-stocked markets. It is usually sold in cylindrical logs.
* Depending on the firmness of the particular goat cheese you buy, it may be cut into thin disks or simply crumbled and dotted on the tortillas by hand.
* Damson jam, made from a tart-sweet plum variety, may be found in well-stocked markets. If you can't find it, substitute another type of plum jam or preserves, or a similarly tart-sweet apricot jam or preserves.

chili-cheese quesadillas

A smear of hot pepper sauce and a crumble of *queso fresco,* fresh Mexican white cheese, make a simple but eloquent grilled quesadilla to serve as an appetizer, a light lunch dish, or as an accompaniment to other grilled foods.

———— 4 servings ————

4 large flour tortillas

2 tablespoons extra-virgin olive oil

1 to 2 teaspoons hot pepper sauce

¾ pound mild white fresh Mexican cheese, crumbled

Preheat the grill.

Just before cooking, brush both sides of each tortilla with olive oil. Carefully oil the grill rack and place the tortillas on the grill. With a long-handled knife or spatula or the back of a long-handled spoon, immediately spread the pepper sauce over the entire top of each tortilla and then quickly scatter the cheese over half of the surface. With tongs, immediately fold the other half of the tortilla over the cheese. Cook until the cheese has melted and the tortillas are golden brown on both sides, turning once, 3 to 4 minutes total cooking time.

With the tongs or a spatula, remove the quesadillas from the grill. Transfer the quesadillas to a cutting board and, with a sharp knife, cut into wedges.

quick tips & variations

* If you can't find mild, crumbly white Mexican cheese in the refrigerated case of your market, substitute mild feta cheese.
* Any popular brand of bottled hot sauce will work well, from Tabasco sauce to an imported Mexican brand such as Cholula, my favorite. Also excellent is Sriracha, the popular bottled Asian pepper sauce flavored with garlic.
* If you like, add a little finely chopped fresh cilantro or chives, or some crumbled dried oregano, along with the cheese.

provoleta

Argentine steak houses serve griddle-seared slices of provolone cheese as a popular appetizer. Two thin slices of good rustic or sourdough bread transform this traditional dish into a grill specialty—and, in the process, make perfect sense, as provoleta is usually served with crusty bread.

— 4 servings —

1 ½-inch-thick slice provolone cheese, about 4 ounces

2 ¼-inch-thick center slices cut from a large, round loaf of dense-crumbed rustic or sourdough bread

¼ teaspoon dried oregano

1 tablespoon extra-virgin olive oil

3 firm, ripe Roma tomatoes, cored, seeded, and coarsely chopped

½ sweet onion, finely chopped

1 tablespoon finely chopped Italian parsley

1 tablespoon thinly shredded fresh basil

Salt

Black pepper

Preheat the grill.

Meanwhile, prepare the provoleta. Using the slice of cheese as a template, cut each bread slice to the same size and shape. Assemble the bread and cheese into a sandwich, crumbling the dried oregano over both sides of the cheese as you do. Pour the olive oil onto a plate and dip both sides of the sandwich into the oil to coat the bread, leaving the sandwich on the plate.

In a mixing bowl, toss together the tomatoes, onion, parsley, and basil. Season to taste with salt and black pepper and set aside.

Carefully oil the grill rack. Place the provoleta on the grill and cook until golden brown and crusty on both sides, 4 to 5 minutes total, carefully turning once with a spatula. Transfer the provoleta to the plate on which it sat, cut it into quarters, and transfer them to individual serving plates. Heap the tomato salad on top and serve immediately.

quick tips & variations

* If the provolone is not available in a single thick slice, buy an equivalent weight of packaged slices. Carefully remove any paper that separates them, then restack them to a ½-inch thickness.
* It's crucial to select a firm-crumbed bread loaf big enough to yield slices at least slightly larger than the cheese's dimensions.
* Chimichurri, a sauce traditionally served with grilled Argentine steak (see page 51), also makes an excellent accompaniment. Or coat the provoleta with chimichurri instead of olive oil before grilling.
* Anchovy paste is also delicious smeared inside the bread along with the oregano.

extra-crunchy grilled cheese and bacon sandwiches

Now here's a novel concept: grilled cheese actually cooked on a grill! These sandwiches make a nice casual lunch, and are particularly handy to prepare if you have a gas grill or an indoor grill.

— 4 servings —

8 slices good-quality white sandwich bread

6 tablespoons unsalted butter, softened

8 strips smoked bacon, each cut in half

8 ounces shredded sharp Cheddar, Monterey Jack, or other good-quality melting cheese

quicktips & variations

* If you keep your sliced bread sealed in a plastic bag in the freezer, as we do in our home, you'll find that it's even easier and quicker to spread with the softened butter.
* Handle the bacon carefully to safeguard against pieces' slipping through the grill rack and into the fire. If your bacon has a trace of rind, nick the edges of the strips with a knife tip to prevent curling. If your rack is widely spaced, don't cut the strips in half until after they've cooked.
* Vary the cheeses according to your taste, or use a mix of cheeses.
* If you like, quickly spread the first toasted sides of the bread with a little Dijon mustard or sour plum jam before doing the final assembly of the sandwiches on the grill.

Preheat the grill.

Meanwhile, prepare the bread slices, spreading each slice evenly on both sides with the butter. Set them aside and have the bacon ready on a separate plate and the cheese ready in a bowl.

Carefully oil the grill rack. Arrange the bacon strips perpendicular to the bars of the rack so that they can't fall through and grill them just until light golden brown and crisp, turning them once, about 4 to 5 minutes total cooking time. Remove them from the grill and set them aside.

Place the bread slices on the grill to begin toasting. As soon as their undersides are golden brown, after 1 to 2 minutes, immediately flip them over and spread the cheese on top of half of the slices. Top the cheese with the bacon and the other bread slices, toasted side down.

Continue grilling, pressing down with a spatula to help seal the sandwiches as the cheese melts, until their undersides are golden, about 2 minutes more. Using the spatula, and holding the top slice of bread in place with another spatula, tongs, or a fork, flip the sandwiches over. Continue grilling, pressing down with the spatula until their undersides are golden brown and the cheese has fully melted, sealing the sandwiches together, 1 to 2 minutes more. Transfer the sandwiches to a cutting board, cut them diagonally into halves or quarters, and serve immediately.

croque-madame on the grill

An egg-enriched cheese sandwich comes out delightfully moist and crunchy when cooked on the grill.

4 servings

Preheat the grill.

Meanwhile, assemble the sandwiches. In a shallow bowl, use a fork to lightly beat the eggs and milk with salt and pepper to taste. One by one, dip both sides of each bread slice in the egg mixture, repeating the process until the bread has soaked up all the egg. Layer the cheeses between the bread slices to make 4 sandwiches, pressing down on each sandwich with your hand to seal it. With a knife, gently spread the softened butter on both sides of each sandwich. Set aside.

Carefully oil the grill rack. Place the sandwiches on the grill and cook, pressing down gently but firmly with a spatula from time to time to help seal them. Turn them once, until the sandwiches are golden brown on both sides, about 10 minutes total. Transfer the sandwiches to a cutting board and cut into halves or quarters.

4 extra-large eggs

2 tablespoons milk

Salt

Black pepper

8 slices rustic bread

3 ounces thinly sliced Cheddar cheese

3 ounces thinly sliced mozzarella cheese

8 tablespoons unsalted butter, softened

quick tips & variations

* Used presliced or even preshredded cheeses for convenience.
* To make a croque-monsieur, lay a thin slice of ham inside each sandwich before grilling.

parmesan garlic toasts

This is a crisp variation on an Italian restaurant favorite. Serve with grilled steaks or lamb or with a tomato salad.

— 4 servings —

6 tablespoons unsalted butter, softened

4 tablespoons freshly grated Parmesan cheese

2 garlic cloves, peeled

8 (½-inch-thick) slices rustic-style bread, each about 4 by 6 inches

Preheat the grill.

Meanwhile, put the butter and Parmesan in a bowl. Press the garlic cloves through a garlic press and into the bowl. With a fork, mash the ingredients together.

With a knife, generously spread the butter-and-cheese mixture over both sides of each bread slice.

Carefully oil the grill rack. Place the bread slices on the grill and cook, turning once, until they are well browned, about 4 minutes total.

quick tips
& variations

* For the right bread, seek out a good-quality whole bakery loaf with a good crust and a firm, dense crumb, such as a rustic Italian loaf or sourdough.
* Use a good, sharp, serrated bread knife to cut the bread. To get the approximate dimensions of the slices called for in the recipe, you may have to slice the loaf on the diagonal, or cut middle slices from a round loaf into halves.

a loaf of rustic bread

One of the most appealing companions to many grilled foods is a loaf of rustic bread with a thick, crunchy-chewy crust and a dense but tender crumb. It slices well into the thin pieces required for the grilled toasts in this chapter. At its simplest, the bread can be sliced to any thickness you like, drizzled with fragrant olive oil, and briefly toasted over the fire.

Good-quality boutique bakeries are among the best sources for such freshly baked loaves. But many good supermarkets today, recognizing the widespread consumer appeal of top-notch baked goods, now distribute boutique breads or make their own loaves. Look for breads whose names or labels include such words as "rustic," "peasant," or "country." Sourdough loaves certainly fall within such categories, and the wild-yeast cultures used to leaven them contribute an added tang that goes well with the edge of smoky flavor from the grill.

rustic garlic toasts

The heat of the grill adds extra dimensions of texture and taste to garlic bread. Serve these toasts as an accompaniment to grilled main courses or with salads to start a meal.

— 4 servings —

4 tablespoons extra-virgin olive oil

2 garlic cloves, peeled

8 (½-inch-thick) slices rustic-style bread, each about 4 by 6 inches

   Salt (optional)

Preheat the grill.

Meanwhile, put the olive oil in a small bowl. Press the garlic cloves through a garlic press and into the bowl. Stir well.

With a basting brush or a small spoon, generously paint the garlic oil over both sides of each bread slice. If you like, lightly sprinkle the bread with salt to taste.

Carefully oil the grill rack. Place the bread slices on the grill and cook, turning once, until they are well browned and crisp, about 4 minutes total.

quick tips & variations

* When grilling large steaks that are cut into slices for guests, drape individual servings over the garlic toasts to make open-faced steak sandwiches. The toasts do an excellent job of soaking up flavorful juices.
* Try substituting walnut or hazelnut oil for half of the olive oil to make toasts that are especially good served with cheese as an hors d'oeuvre or at the end of a grilled meal.

tuscan
pestotoasts

A smear of store-bought pesto, the classic Italian sauce of basil, garlic, pine nuts, Parmesan, and olive oil, adds a heady aroma to this quick accompaniment for grilled meats or poultry.

—— 4 servings ——

Preheat the grill.

With a knife or the back of a spoon, spread the pesto on both sides of each bread slice.

Carefully oil the grill rack. Place the bread slices on the grill and cook, turning once, until they are well browned and crisp, about 4 minutes total.

8 (½-inch-thick) slices rustic-style bread, each about 4 by 6 inches

4 tablespoons prepared pesto

quicktips &variations

* You'll find good-quality, fresh pesto in well-stocked supermarkets, sold in sealed containers in the refrigerated case or in a separate display with other sauces and fresh pastas. If you like, substitute sun-dried tomato pesto or other types of pesto, which are sometimes sold alongside the classic variety.

herb-garlic cream cheese toasts

Commercial garlic-herb cream cheese spreads such as the well-known Boursin change ordinary bread into rich toasts to serve with steaks, seafood, or poultry.

— 4 servings —

8 (½-inch-thick) slices rustic-style bread, each about 4 by 6 inches

1 tablespoon extra-virgin olive oil

4 tablespoons garlic-herb cream cheese, softened

Preheat the grill.

Lightly drizzle the olive oil over one side of each slice of bread.

Carefully oil the grill rack. Place the bread slices oiled side down on the grill rack and cook until their undersides are well browned and crisp, 1½ to 2 minutes. Remove them from the grill and, with a knife or the back of a spoon, quickly spread the garlic-herb cream cheese over their toasted sides. Return the toasts to the grill, cream cheese side up, and cook until their undersides are golden and the cheese is melting, 1½ to 2 minutes more.

quick tips & variations

* You can use fresh, creamy goat cheese in place of the cream cheese spread.
* Plunk a piece of oil-packed sun-dried tomato into the cream cheese on both toasts before returning them to the grill.

naan-style garlic butter pita

You'll be amazed by how this easy recipe transforms store-bought pita bread into a close cousin to the garlic-and-butter-drenched tandoori bread on the menus of Indian restaurants. Serve with any Indian-spiced grilled main course.

— 4 servings

4 pita breads

4 tablespoons unsalted butter, melted

2 garlic cloves, peeled

Salt

Preheat the grill.

Meanwhile, prepare the breads. Stack the pita on a work surface. Put the butter in a small mixing bowl. Press the garlic cloves through a garlic press and into the bowl, stirring together with the butter. With a spoon, smear the garlic butter evenly over both sides of each pita, stacking them onto a plate as you do.

Carefully oil the grill rack. Lightly sprinkle both sides of each pita with salt and put them on the grill. Cook until golden brown, 3 to 4 minutes total, turning once. Stack the pita back on the plate, transfer them to a cutting board and, with a sharp knife, cut the pita into wedges or 2-inch-wide strips. Serve immediately.

quick tips & variations

* Instead of cutting the pita into strips or wedges, cut them into halves before grilling and buttering (most commercial pita have visible perforations to help you do so). Stuff the halves with a grilled main course such as thinly sliced Tandoori-Style Leg of Lamb with Vegetable-Herb Raita (page 80).
* If you'd like a spicier version, stir $1/2$ teaspoon of mild to medium-hot chili powder or sweet or hot paprika into the butter.

grilled polenta with parmesan

1 tube (about 1 pound) prepared polenta or cornmeal mush

¼ cup extra-virgin olive oil

2 tablespoons grated Parmesan cheese

Many Italian delis and upscale markets today sell vacuum-packed, clear plastic tubes of ready-made polenta, which requires only reheating. These are a boon for Quick Grill Artistry, yielding a delicious side dish perfect for Mediterranean-flavored meat or poultry main courses.

———— 4 to 6 servings ————

quick tips & variations

* In some parts of the country, particularly the Midwest and the South, you'll find cornmeal mush packaged in the same way. It will yield similarly good results.
* If you have a little more time and the inclination, you can make the polenta from scratch, following package directions to produce a firm mush. Coat a baking sheet with olive oil and spread the hot polenta to an even thickness of about ³/₄ inch, using a spatula to ensure that its surface is smooth and level. Let the polenta cool and solidify completely before cutting it into squares, rectangles, or diamonds at least 3 inches wide for grilling.
* Substitute shredded mozzarella, crumbled blue cheese, or another favorite melting cheese for the Parmesan (alone or in combination).
* Before adding the cheese, smear a heaping teaspoon of good-quality, store-bought pesto sauce onto each slice.
* If the polenta slices seem at all fragile or crumbly, consider cooking them on a smaller mesh grid placed atop your grill rack.

Preheat the grill.

Meanwhile, prepare the polenta. Unwrap the tube over the sink, draining off any excess liquid. Pat the cylinder of polenta dry with paper towels. On a cutting board, cut the cylinder of polenta at a 45-degree angle into slices about ³/₄ inch thick. Pour the olive oil into a shallow baking dish or tray large enough to hold the polenta slices in a single layer. Carefully turn the polenta in the oil to coat it on both sides.

Carefully oil the grill rack. Place the polenta slices on the grill and cook them until their undersides are golden brown and crusty, 3 to 4 minutes. With a spatula, carefully turn them over. Immediately sprinkle the tops with the Parmesan cheese. Cover and continue grilling until the undersides are golden brown, 3 to 4 minutes more.

quick pizzas on the grill

It may sound odd, but pizzas cook quickly and easily on the grill. The rolled-out dough doesn't droop through the bars of the grill rack, as you might fear. Instead, the dough firms up quickly. The live fire gives it a deliciously charred taste reminiscent of classic pizzas baked in wood-fired ovens, and cheese toppings melt quickly when the grill's lid is closed.

I first tasted grilled pizza at the outstanding Al Forno restaurant in Providence, Rhode Island, where owners/chefs George Germon and Johanne Killeen justifiably claim to have pioneered the technique. And I was first introduced to the details of that technique by my friend Ethan Becker in the 1997 edition of his three-generation family masterwork, *The Joy of Cooking*. I've adapted that approach to my own style of quick grilling, and offer the following suggestions to help you achieve success:

* Most supermarkets carry ready-to-bake raw bread dough in the frozen food section, as well as vacuum-packed yeast-leavened bread or pizza doughs in the refrigerated case. If necessary, let the dough defrost following package instructions before you begin the recipe.
* Note that some refrigerated-case pizza doughs may be soda-leavened rather than yeast-leavened, and may contain a smaller quantity of dough than the 1 pound called for in my recipes. Soda-leavened doughs will be softer in consistency, demanding more delicate handling and careful turning. Adjust topping quantities proportionately to the amount of dough you use.
* If your grill surface isn't large enough, or you'd feel more comfortable handling smaller pizzas, divide the dough and toppings into batches.
* Read over the recipe before you start cooking. Have the dough, its toppings, and the tools you'll use all ready and arrayed around the grill before you begin cooking. Things move quickly once the dough hits the grill rack.
* Don't worry if the dough becomes misshapen or you don't distribute the toppings evenly. The pizza will only look more appealingly rustic—and your skills will have sharpened by the time you make your second or third grilled pizza.

three-cheese garlic grilled pizza

Here's something fast and flavorful to enjoy while the main course is cooking on the grill. It can also become a great main course in its own right.

————— 4 to 8 servings —————

4 tablespoons extra-virgin olive oil

1 garlic clove, peeled

1 pound ready-to-bake pizza dough or other yeast bread dough, defrosted if necessary

¼ pound shredded mozzarella cheese

2 ounces shredded fontina cheese

¼ cup grated Parmesan cheese

1 tablespoon dried oregano

1 tablespoon finely shredded fresh basil

Preheat the grill under only one side of the grill rack.

Meanwhile, prepare the pizza ingredients. Put the olive oil in a small bowl and press the garlic clove through a garlic press and into the oil. Stir well. Drizzle half of the oil onto a large rimmed baking sheet, reserving the remainder. Turn the dough in the oil on the baking sheet to coat it, then gently press and pull the dough on the sheet, taking care not to tear it. Continue until you have stretched it out into a large, thin circle or rectangle that will fit on half of your grill rack's surface. In another bowl, toss together the mozzarella, fontina, Parmesan, oregano, and basil. Set aside.

Carefully oil the cooler side of the grill rack, away from the fire. Lift the pizza dough by one edge and drape it onto the cooler side of the grill rack. Immediately cover the grill. After 2 to 3 minutes, check the dough; as soon as it is stiff and you can begin to see grill marks through it, carefully use tongs to flip the dough over. Immediately brush the remaining oil over the dough and spread the cheese mixture evenly on top. Cover the grill and continue cooking until the cheese has melted, 5 to 7 minutes more.

Use a pair of large spatulas or a baker's peel to remove the pizza from the grill and transfer it to the baking sheet or a cutting board. With a pizza wheel or a large, sharp knife, cut the pizza into wedges or squares.

quick tips & variations

* If you like, substitute a flavored olive oil infused with such seasonings as basil or sun-dried tomatoes.
* Feel free to vary the mixture of cheeses with whatever strikes your fancy.

grilled pizza with sun-dried tomato oil and pepper jack

Favorite California flavors enhance this grilled pizza.
—— 4 to 8 servings ——

Preheat the grill under only one side of the grill rack.

Meanwhile, prepare the pizza ingredients. Drizzle half of the sun-dried tomato oil onto a large rimmed baking sheet, reserving the remainder. Turn the dough in the oil on the baking sheet to coat it, then gently press and pull the dough on the sheet, taking care not to tear it. Continue until you have stretched it out into a large, thin circle or rectangle that will fit on half of your grill rack's surface. In another bowl, toss together the pepper Jack and mozzarella cheeses and the sun-dried tomato slivers. Set aside.

Carefully oil the cooler side of the grill rack, away from the fire. Lift the pizza dough by one edge and drape it onto the cooler side of the grill rack. Immediately cover the grill. After 2 to 3 minutes, check the dough; as soon as it is stiff and you can begin to see grill marks through it, carefully use tongs to flip the dough over. Immediately brush the remaining oil over the dough and spread the cheese mixture evenly on top. Cover the grill and continue cooking until the cheese has melted, 5 to 7 minutes more.

Use a pair of large spatulas or a baker's peel to remove the pizza from the grill and transfer it to the baking sheet or a cutting board. With a pizza wheel or a large, sharp knife, cut the pizza into wedges or squares. If you wish, scatter the basil on top.

4 tablespoons oil drained from a jar of sun-dried tomatoes

1 pound ready-to-bake pizza dough or other yeast bread dough, defrosted if necessary

¼ pound pepper Jack cheese, shredded

2 ounces shredded mozzarella cheese

12 sun-dried tomatoes, cut into ¼-inch-wide slivers

2 tablespoons finely shredded fresh basil (optional)

quicktips &variations

* This flavor combination works very well with seafood. Try scattering $1/2$ pound of cooked and peeled baby bay shrimp, found in your market's seafood case, over the pizza just before you add the cheese mixture.

smoked salmon grilled pizza

Wolfgang Puck first came up with the brilliant idea of topping just-baked pizza dough with smoked salmon. Grilled pizza at its most elegant, this deserves to be served with your favorite sparkling wine to start a special grilled meal.

— 4 to 8 servings —

2 tablespoons extra-virgin olive oil

1 pound ready-to-bake pizza dough or other yeast bread dough, defrosted if necessary

¼ pound whipped cream cheese

½ pound smoked salmon, thinly sliced

2 tablespoons finely chopped fresh chives

Lemon wedges

Preheat the grill under only one side of the grill rack.

Meanwhile, prepare the pizza ingredients. Drizzle the oil onto a large rimmed baking sheet. Turn the dough in the oil on the baking sheet to coat it, then gently press and pull the dough on the sheet, taking care not to tear it. Continue until you have stretched it out into a large, thin circle or rectangle that will fit on half of your grill rack's surface. Set aside.

Carefully oil the cooler side of the grill rack, away from the fire. Lift the pizza dough by one edge and drape it onto the cooler side of the grill rack. Immediately cover the grill. After 2 to 3 minutes, check the dough; as soon as it is stiff and you can begin to see grill marks through it, use tongs to carefully flip the dough over. Using the back of a long-handled spoon, immediately spread the cream cheese over the dough. Cover the grill and continue cooking until the underside of the dough is browned and crisp, 4 to 5 minutes more.

Use a pair of large spatulas or a baker's peel to remove the pizza from the grill and transfer it to the baking sheet or a cutting board. Drape the smoked salmon slices evenly on top of the cream cheese. With a pizza wheel or a large, sharp knife, cut the pizza into wedges or squares. Sprinkle it with the chives and serve with lemon wedges for each guest to squeeze over the pizza, if desired.

quick tips & variations

* Many stores today carry good-quality, vacuum-packed, presliced smoked salmon in their refrigerated case, often at excellent value.
* Add 1 clove of garlic, pressed through a garlic press, to the olive oil.
* Use a garlic-and-herb-flavored commercial cream cheese in place of the plain cream cheese.
* Substitute dill for the chives. Or scatter drained small capers over the salmon along with the herbs.
* Freshly ground black pepper nicely complements smoked salmon. Pass a pepper mill for guests to add it, if desired.

classic cheese and tomato grilled pizza

Sometimes nothing will do but the classic pizzeria combination. Good results are made easy by using premade, good-quality pizza sauce or marinara sauce, found in the refrigerated case or the canned goods aisle of the market.

— 4 to 8 servings —

Preheat the grill under only one side of the grill rack.

Meanwhile, prepare the pizza ingredients. Drizzle the olive oil onto a large rimmed baking sheet. Turn the dough in the oil on the baking sheet to coat it, then gently press and pull the dough on the sheet, taking care not to tear it. Continue until you have stretched it out into a large, thin circle or rectangle that will fit on half of your grill rack's surface. Put the sauce in a bowl and have a long-handled spoon ready for spreading it. Put the Parmesan in a small bowl, with a spoon for sprinkling it. In another bowl, toss together the mozzarella and oregano. Set aside.

Carefully oil the cooler side of the grill rack, away from the fire. Lift the pizza dough by one edge and drape it onto the cooler side of the grill rack. Immediately cover the grill. After 2 to 3 minutes, check the dough; as soon as it is stiff and you can begin to see grill marks through it, use tongs to carefully flip the dough over. Immediately spread the sauce over the dough, sprinkle evenly with the Parmesan, and then scatter the mozzarella on top. Cover the grill and continue cooking until the cheese has melted, 5 to 7 minutes more.

Use a pair of large spatulas or a baker's peel to remove the pizza from the grill and transfer it to a cutting board or clean baking sheet. With a pizza wheel or a large, sharp knife, cut the pizza into wedges or squares.

2 tablespoons extra-virgin olive oil

1 pound ready-to-bake pizza dough or other yeast bread dough, defrosted if necessary

¾ cup pizza sauce or marinara sauce

¼ cup grated Parmesan cheese

6 ounces shredded mozzarella cheese

2 teaspoons dried oregano

quick tips & variations

* Taste the sauce for seasoning ahead of time. If it tastes a little flat and without a good tomatoey character, stir in up to a teaspoon of sugar. Likewise, if it doesn't have a good edge of herbal flavor, stir in up to a teaspoon of dried oregano.
* Substitute good-quality, store-bought pesto for the pizza sauce or marinara sauce. Or use a mixture of pesto and tomato-based sauces.
* Feel free to add other favorite cheeses.
* Add thinly sliced pepperoni sausage or ham before you sprinkle on the mozzarella. You can also grill strips of bacon or links of Italian sausage beforehand and crumble them over the sauce.

feta cheese wrapped in grape leaves

Here's another quick, easy, and elegant solution to cooking cheese on the grill: wrapping bite-sized pieces in individual, edible grape leaves. These make an impressive first course.

—— 4 servings ——

¾-pound block feta cheese

4 tablespoons extra-virgin olive oil

2 teaspoons dried oregano

12 bottled grape leaves, rinsed and drained on paper towels

1 lemon, cut into 4 wedges

Preheat the grill.

Meanwhile, prepare the cheese. Cut the block of feta into 12 equal pieces, each about 1 by 2 inches. Place them on paper towels to drain. In a shallow dish, pour the olive oil and then crumble in the oregano. Add the feta pieces to the oil and turn them gently to coat them. One at a time, put a grape leaf on a work surface, with its stem end closest to you and the tip pointing upward. Place a piece of feta horizontally across the widest part of the leaf. Fold the two sides over the ends of the cheese; then, fold the stem end up over the cheese and continue rolling the bundle upward to enclose the cheese completely. Return the package to the oil and turn to coat the leaf and seal it. Repeat with the remaining grape leaves and cheese.

Carefully oil the grill rack. Put the feta packages on the grill at right angles to the wires of the rack and grill, carefully turning once with tongs or a spatula. Continue until the leaves are lightly charred and the packages sag and ooze slightly, indicating the feta is melting, about 3 minutes in all. Remove to a serving platter or individual plates and serve immediately with the lemon wedges.

quick tips & variations

* I prefer a milder-tasting feta for this recipe. But if your tastes run to the more tangy end of the flavor spectrum, feel free to use the kind of feta you like.
* Fresh or dried dill also works well with the feta.
* These little cheese bundles may be eaten with the fingers or with a knife and fork.
* Crusty bread makes a great accompaniment.

grilled
camembert
salad

The powdery white rind of a Camembert makes it possible to heat this cheese whole on the grill in a matter of minutes, turning the soft interior enticingly warm and runny. Cut into wedges after grilling, the cheese is outstanding served atop mixed baby greens as the centerpiece of a simple salad to start a special outdoor meal.

———— 4 servings ————

Preheat the grill.

Meanwhile, prepare the cheese and the dressing. Put the whole Camembert on a plate and rub the cheese all over with 1 tablespoon of the olive oil. Set aside.

For the dressing, put the lemon juice in a large salad bowl, add the sugar, salt, and pepper, and stir with a whisk or wooden spoon until the sugar and salt dissolve. Stir in the mustard. Stirring continuously and briskly, slowly drizzle in the remaining olive oil to form a thick dressing. Pile the salad greens atop the dressing but do not toss. Set aside.

Carefully oil the grill rack. Place the cheese on the side of the grill, slightly away from the hottest part of the fire, and grill until the rind is golden and the cheese appears to droop slightly, 2 to 3 minutes total. Carefully turn the cheese once with a metal spatula.

Return the cheese to its plate. Quickly toss the salad greens with the dressing and pile them on individual serving plates. With a sharp knife, cut the cheese into 4 equal wedges and place a wedge atop the greens on each plate. Serve immediately.

1 small whole, ripe Camembert cheese (about 8 ounces)

5 tablespoons extra-virgin olive oil

2 tablespoons lemon juice

¼ teaspoon sugar

⅛ teaspoon salt

⅛ teaspoon black pepper

2 teaspoons regular or coarse-grained Dijon mustard

4 cups mixed baby salad greens

quicktips
&variations

* You'll find whole Camembert cheeses, usually in circular cardboard boxes, in the cheese department of most markets. If you can, gently prod the cheese with your fingertips: It should feel firm but yield slightly, an indication of ripeness.
* Buy ready-to-use bags of mixed salad greens, now widely available.
* If you like, garnish each serving with a teaspoon or two of finely chopped fresh chives.

meat

For many outdoor cooks, grilling and meat are one and the same, whether the main course sizzling over the fire is a steak, a burger, a hot dog, a sausage, a pork chop, or a lamb chop. The Quick Grill Artist simply knows how to elevate that familiar fare above the ordinary with a quick sauce, an easy and intense marinade or glaze, a rapid injection of flavor, or some thoughtfully (but nonetheless quickly) chosen accompaniments.

Whatever path you take to elaborate meat on the grill, your most important decision is the meat you buy. Look for top-quality products from a reliable butcher, whether in an upscale supermarket or an independent shop. Choose tender, flavorful cuts that are thin enough to cook fairly quickly to your desired degree of doneness.

Regarding that topic, I highly recommend that you buy a good-quality, instant-read meat thermometer, widely available in kitchen equipment stores and even in the kitchen supply aisles of some well-stocked supermarkets. Alternatively, look for a long-handled, two-pronged grilling fork with a built-in, battery-operated doneness gauge. Either tool will help you achieve your desired degree of doneness without the need to cut into, and thus mar the presentation of, the food you're grilling.

cowboy steaks with redeye chili rub

This rich-tasting rub takes its unusual name from old-fashioned "redeye" gravy, a chuck wagon favorite made by using black coffee to deglaze the pan in which ham steaks had cooked. There's no discernible coffee taste when the steaks come off the grill—just a distinctive richness that enhances the flavors of good beef and mild chili powder.

———— 4 servings ————

Preheat the grill. Trim excess fat from the steaks and set them aside at room temperature.

While the grill is heating, make the redeye rub. In a small bowl, stir together the chili powder, onion salt, cumin, sugar, and black pepper. Add the coffee and butter and stir to form a paste. Rub the paste on both sides of the steaks.

Carefully oil the grill rack. Place the steaks on the rack and cook, turning once, until done to your liking, 16 to 20 minutes total for medium-rare.

4 ribeye, T-bone, or New York steaks (10 to 12 ounces each)

2 tablespoons mild to medium-hot pure chili powder

1 tablespoon onion salt

2 teaspoons ground cumin

1 teaspoon sugar

1 teaspoon freshly ground black pepper

2 tablespoons brewed strong black coffee

2 tablespoons unsalted butter, melted

quick tips & variations

* Use any other good-quality steak of your choice. The rub also works well with pork chops.
* If you plan ahead to make this recipe, refrigerate a splash of coffee from your morning brew.
* Fire-Licked Guacamole (page 161) makes a wonderful accompaniment.

prime cuts

Do you ever wonder why steaks in a great steak house seem to taste far better than anything you could ever grill at home? The main reason is that steak houses buy the very best grade of beef available: well-aged, tender, USDA Prime cuts from the finest steers, with outstanding marbling of flavorful fat throughout the meat. By contrast, the best grades sold by most markets are Choice or Select, still good but one or two notches below in flavor and tenderness.

Some few butchers do, however, sell Prime beef. Look up the best shops in your area in the classified phone directory, and call them to see if it's available. Or ask the butcher in a full-service supermarket if it can be ordered. You'll pay more, but you'll come that much closer to steak-house flavor.

If you can't find Prime beef, however, don't despair. Choice and Select cuts can still taste great, and the recipes on these pages will help ensure that you get the highest artistry from your quick grilling efforts.

argentine steaks with quick chimichurri

The classic Argentine salsa doubles as both seasoning and table condiment for good-quality beefsteaks.

——————————— 4 servings ——

4 1½-inch beefsteaks,
   1 to 1½ pounds total

chimichurri

4 garlic cloves, peeled

½ teaspoon crushed red pepper flakes

2 teaspoons dried oregano

   Salt

   Freshly ground black pepper

¼ cup good-quality red wine vinegar

2 teaspoons lemon juice

½ cup extra-virgin olive oil

⅓ cup minced onion (about ½ small onion)

⅓ cup packed, finely chopped fresh Italian parsley

Preheat the grill. Trim excess fat from the steaks and set them aside at room temperature.

While the grill is heating, make the Chimichurri. Press the garlic cloves through a garlic press and into a mixing bowl. Add the red pepper flakes, oregano, and about ¼ teaspoon each of salt and black pepper. Pressing down with the back of a soupspoon, mash them together with the garlic. With a fork or small whisk, stir in the vinegar and lemon juice. Stirring briskly, drizzle in the olive oil until combined. Stir in the onion and parsley and set aside.

When the grill is ready, lightly coat the steaks on both sides with a little of the Chimichurri. (Take care not to contaminate the sauce with any utensil that has touched the meat.) Season the steaks generously with salt and black pepper to taste.

Carefully oil the grill rack. Place the steaks on the rack and cook, turning once, until done to your liking, 16 to 20 minutes total for medium-rare. Serve the steaks, passing around the Chimichurri for guests to use as a condiment.

quick tips & variations

* Use any good-quality steak.
* Substitute lamb, chicken, or seafood.
* The quantities here also yield a little extra Chimichurri that you can brush onto rustic bread before quickly grilling it (see Rustic Garlic Toasts, page 36), or use as a dip.
* Substitute fresh basil for the parsley.
* If you are preparing the recipe in larger quantities, make the Chimichurri in a food processor. Use the stainless steel blade to mince the garlic and then chop the parsley and onion before pulsing in the other ingredients.

cuban steaks with garlic-citrus marinade and orange-onion salsa

Cuban cooks often add dynamic flavor to meat with a combination of garlic and citrus juice. Here, that combination is further highlighted by a quickly made salsa combining zesty and pungent flavors.

— 4 servings —

4 top round or flank steaks
   (5–6 ounces each)

3 or 4 garlic cloves, peeled

½ cup orange juice

¼ cup lemon juice

2 tablespoons olive oil

orange-onion salsa

2 large, sweet oranges

½ red onion, thinly sliced

2 tablespoons finely chopped
   fresh cilantro

   Salt

   Black pepper

Preheat the grill.

Meanwhile, prepare the steaks. Trim any excess fat or connective tissue from them. One at a time, place each steak piece between two sheets of waxed paper and pound with a meat pounder until they are flattened to a thickness of about ½ inch.

Press the garlic cloves through a garlic press and put into a large, shallow dish. Add the orange and lemon juices and the olive oil and stir well. Add the steaks, turning them in the mixture to coat them, and leave them in the dish at room temperature.

To prepare the Orange-Onion Salsa, segment the oranges. Using a sharp knife, first cut off the peel at the top and bottom of each orange, cutting thickly enough to remove the outer membrane of the orange segments as well. Then stand each orange on a cut end and cut off the peel in strips in the same way. Holding the peeled orange over a bowl to catch the juices, free each segment by cutting between it and the membranes on either side; cut the freed segment crosswise in half and let the halves drop into the bowl. Add the sliced onion and cilantro and toss well, seasoning with salt and pepper to taste.

Carefully oil the grill rack. Remove the steaks from their marinade, pat them dry, and season them with salt and pepper to taste. Place the steaks on the rack and cook, turning once, until done to your liking, 12 to 15 minutes total for medium. Serve the steaks, passing around the Orange-Onion Salsa for guests to spoon alongside the meat.

quick tips
& variations

* Ask the butcher to trim and pound the steaks for you.
* Try the marinade or salsa with grilled lamb, pork, or chicken.
* In place of the red onion, use sweet yellow onions such as Maui, Walla Walla, Vidalia, or Texas 1015s.
* Cook up some white rice mixed with canned black beans, seasoned to taste with a little minced garlic or chopped onion, to serve alongside the steak and salsa in traditional Cuban style.
* Alternatively, briefly warm corn or flour tortillas on the grill to use as wrappers for strips of the steak and spoonfuls of the salsa.

florentine beef steaks with garlic, olive oil, and lemon

It doesn't take much effort to prepare a classic *bistecca alla fiorentina,* which arrives on the plate brimming with flavor and juices.

— 4 servings —

4   T-bone steaks (¾ to 1 pound each)

2   garlic cloves, cut in halves

¼   cup extra-virgin olive oil

Salt

Black pepper

2   lemons, cut in halves

quick tips & variations

* You can prepare other types of steak in the same way, but a bone-in steak works especially well for rubbing and pureeing the garlic.
* I find that sea salt, instead of regular table salt, adds a wonderful extra touch of flavor to this simple preparation.
* Accompany with one of the grilled toast recipes on pages 28–39, as well as with your choice of the potatoes on pages 144–148.
* A simple mixed green salad with a lemon and olive oil dressing goes especially well with these steaks.

Preheat the grill.

Meanwhile, prepare the steaks. Trim any excess fat from their edges. Rub both sides of each steak all over with the cut side of one garlic clove half. Rub it repeatedly and firmly against the bone to puree the garlic, then spread the garlic over the meat. Drizzle the olive oil all over both sides of the steaks and gently rub it into the meat, making sure it is spread evenly.

Carefully oil the grill rack. Season the steaks generously on both sides with salt and black pepper to taste. Grill the steaks, turning once, until done to your liking, about 10 minutes for medium. Transfer the steaks to individual serving plates and immediately squeeze a lemon half over each steak.

three-peppercorn steaks

The fancy restaurant favorite works exceedingly well on the grill, yielding aromatic and flavorful results with minimal effort.

4 servings

Preheat the grill.

Meanwhile, prepare the steaks. In a small bowl, stir together the olive oil and mustard. Place the steaks on a platter or dish large enough to hold them side by side and rub both sides of each steak with the oil-mustard mixture.

Put all the peppercorns in a sturdy plastic bag and place the bag on a work surface. With a meat pounder or rolling pin, crush the peppercorns into coarse particles resembling very fine gravel. Sprinkle the peppercorn mixture on both sides of each steak, pressing it firmly into the meat with your hand.

Carefully oil the grill rack. Season the steaks generously with salt to taste. Place them on the grill rack and cook, turning them once, until done to your liking, 12 to 14 minutes total cooking time for medium. Remove from the heat and serve immediately.

2 tablespoons extra-virgin olive oil

2 tablespoons Dijon mustard

4 ¾-to-1-inch-thick sirloin steaks (about 9 ounces each)

1 tablespoon whole black peppercorns

1 tablespoon whole red peppercorns

1 tablespoon whole white peppercorns

Salt

quick tips & variations

* Substitute your favorite steaks for the sirloins in this recipe. It also works spectacularly well with hamburgers.
* You'll find whole peppercorns of all colors in the spice section of a well-stocked supermarket. Feel free to substitute or add green peppercorns, or to use fewer than three kinds if necessary.
* Serve with grilled onions or mushrooms of your choice.

steaks with chipotle-garlic chili butter

The rich, not-too-hot flavor of smoke-dried jalapeño chili peppers adds Southwestern savor to these steaks.

— 4 servings —

4 1-to-1½-inch-thick sirloin or
New York steaks,
10 to 12 ounces each

4 tablespoons unsalted butter,
softened

1 canned chipotle chili in adobo
sauce, finely chopped

1 teaspoon adobo sauce from
canned chipotle chilies

1 garlic clove, peeled

Salt

Black pepper

Preheat the grill.

Meanwhile, prepare the steaks and chili butter. Trim excess fat from the steaks and set them aside at room temperature. Put the unsalted butter, chipotle chili, and adobo sauce in a mixing bowl. Press the garlic clove through a garlic press and into the bowl. Using a fork, mash together the ingredients. Set aside.

Carefully oil the grill rack. Season the steaks generously with salt and black pepper to taste. Place the steaks on the grill and cook, turning once, until done to your liking, 14 to 18 minutes for medium. Transfer the steaks to serving plates and immediately top each with a dollop of the chili butter.

quick tips & variations

* The chili butter is excellent with any kind of steak and is also good with chicken or meaty seafood such as swordfish, halibut, or sea bass. Adjust the amount of chili butter you place on top of each portion, according to its size.
* You'll find small cans of chipotle chilies immersed in tomato-based adobo sauce in well-stocked food stores and Latino markets. Transfer the remaining contents of the can to an airtight container and refrigerate; they'll keep well for up to a week.
* Add chopped fresh cilantro or chives to the butter mixture; or sprinkle the herbs over each butter-topped steak at serving time.

meat

56

steaks with black pepper parmesan butter

These simply prepared steaks possess a flavor sophisticated enough to merit a good red wine.

4 servings

Preheat the grill.

Meanwhile, prepare the steaks and the Parmesan butter. Trim excess fat from the steaks and set them aside at room temperature. For the Parmesan butter, put the unsalted butter, Parmesan, and black pepper in a small bowl. With a fork, mash them together. Set aside.

Carefully oil the grill rack. Season the steaks generously with salt to taste. Place the steaks on the grill rack and cook, turning once, until done to your liking, 14 to 18 minutes for medium. Transfer the steaks to serving plates and immediately top each with a dollop of the Parmesan butter.

4 1-to-1½-inch-thick sirloin or New York steaks (10 to 12 ounces each)

4 tablespoons unsalted butter, softened

1½ tablespoons grated Parmesan cheese

½ tablespoon coarsely ground black pepper

Salt

quick tips & variations

* Try substituting crumbled blue cheese such as Gorgonzola, Stilton, or Roquefort for the Parmesan.
* Add a chopped fresh herb such as chives or parsley to the butter mixture, or sprinkle the herbs over each butter-topped steak at serving time.
* Instead of grinding the pepper by hand, feel free to use coarsely ground black pepper from a jar.

meat

steaks with sun-dried tomato basil butter

This butter's intense tomato flavor complements steak in the same way that a great steak sauce does.

— 4 servings —

- 4 1-to-1½-inch-thick sirloin or New York steaks (10 to 12 ounces each)
- 4 tablespoons unsalted butter, softened
- 4 to 6 oil-packed sun-dried tomatoes, finely chopped (about 2 generous tablespoons total)
- 1 tablespoon finely chopped fresh basil leaves
- ¼ teaspoon sugar

   Salt

   Black pepper

Preheat the grill.

Meanwhile, prepare the steaks and the tomato-basil butter. Trim excess fat from the steaks and set them aside at room temperature. For the tomato-basil butter, put the unsalted butter, sun-dried tomatoes, basil, and sugar in a small bowl. With a fork, mash them together. Set aside.

Carefully oil the grill rack. Season the steaks generously with salt and black pepper to taste. Place the steaks on the grill rack and cook, turning once, until done to your liking, 14 to 18 minutes for medium. Transfer the steaks to serving plates and immediately top each with a dollop of the tomato-basil butter.

quick tips & variations

* You can find sun-dried tomatoes in most supermarkets today. They usually come packed in olive oil, which picks up the flavor of the tomatoes and is worth using in its own right.
* If only dry-packed sun-dried tomatoes in plastic bags are available, soak them in hot water to cover until soft, about 10 minutes, then drain before chopping them.

self-basting garlic-pepper steak

Many meat lovers desire their steaks steeped in garlic flavor. An injection of garlic-scented olive oil achieves that goal admirably, and it also serves to baste a bigger steak, such as a whole tri-tip or sirloin, from the inside out.

4 servings

Preheat the grill.

Meanwhile, prepare the steak. Trim excess fat from the meat and put it in a shallow dish. Pour the olive oil into a small bowl. Press the garlic cloves through a garlic press and into the oil. Add a few generous shakes of salt and grindings of black pepper and stir the oil mixture. Transfer the oil to a meat syringe and carefully plunge the syringe deep into the meat at its thickest point until the tip almost reaches the other side. Then, slowly pull out the syringe while slowly pressing down on the plunger to inject about half of the seasoned oil along the inside of the steak. In the same way, inject the rest of the oil in various other parts of the steak.

Carefully oil the grill rack. Season the steak generously all over with salt and a generous amount of black pepper to taste. Place the steak on the grill and cook it until it is evenly well seared all over with grill marks, about 3 minutes per side. Move it closer to the side of the grill and continue cooking until the steak is done to your liking, 20 to 25 minutes more for medium. Turn the steak once halfway through. A meat thermometer inserted into the thickest part should register 135°F.

Remove the steak from the heat to a serving platter, cover it loosely with foil, and let it sit for about 5 minutes before carving it across the grain into ¼-inch-thick slices.

1½ to 2 pounds tri-tip, sirloin, or top round steak, in one piece

2 tablespoons extra-virgin olive oil

2 garlic cloves, peeled

Salt

Black pepper

quicktips & variations

* To cut grilling time by about half, substitute smaller individual steaks of your choice about 1 inch thick. Injecting the oil, however, will become a slightly trickier proposition, requiring you to insert the syringe needle carefully at various points along the side of the steak and perfectly parallel to its surface.
* Add a little very finely minced basil or parsley to the oil mixture, taking care that no pieces are big enough to clog the syringe.
* Serve with your choice of grilled potatoes (pages 144–148). Or drape the steak slices over your choice of grilled toasts (pages 28–39).

flank steak fajitas on the grill

The Mexican restaurant favorite is exceedingly easy to make—and exceptionally delicious when grilled. The quick cooking, followed by thin slicing across the grain, brings tenderness to a chewy, less expensive cut of beef. Accompany, if you like, with Fire-Licked Guacamole (page 161) and Fire-Roasted Chili-Tomato Salsa (page 162).

———— 4 to 6 servings ————

1½ pounds flank steak

1 teaspoon mild to medium-hot pure chili powder

½ teaspoon ground cumin

Salt

Black pepper

2 red, yellow, or green bell peppers, quartered, stemmed, seeded

1 yellow or red onion, cut into ½-inch-thick slices

¼ cup extra-virgin olive oil

12 corn tortillas

2 limes, cut into wedges

Preheat the grill.

Meanwhile, trim any excess fat or connective tissue from the surface of the steak. Put the steak in a large, shallow container and sprinkle it on both sides with the chili powder, cumin, and salt and black pepper to taste. Add the bell pepper quarters to the dish. Insert two or three sturdy wooden toothpicks sideways into each onion slice to secure the rings, then add the onions to the dish. Drizzle the olive oil evenly all over both sides of the steak, peppers, and onions. Set aside.

Carefully oil the grill rack. Add the steak, bell pepper quarters, and onions. Grill the vegetables until they are tender and nicely browned on both sides, even slightly charred, 8 to 10 minutes total. Remove them to a clean serving dish and cover them with foil while the steak continues grilling. Cook the steak, turning once, until done to your liking, 15 to 17 minutes for medium. Remove the steak from the grill to a cutting board and cover it with foil to keep warm. Warm the tortillas on the grill, turning them once, just until they soften and give off an aroma of corn. Remove them from the grill when they are done, stacking them on a plate and covering them with foil.

In the kitchen, quickly squeeze a couple of wedges of lime all over the steak. With a sharp knife, cut the steak across the grain into ¼-inch-thick strips. Remove the toothpicks from the onion slices and cut each slice in half. Cut the peppers into ¼-inch-thick strips. Toss the steak strips and the vegetables together and serve, passing the fajita mixture and the tortillas for guests to make their own soft tacos.

quick tips
& variations

* Any other thin cuts of steak, such as top round or London broil, may be used in place of the flank steak.
* If you don't want to go to the trouble of making your own guacamole or salsa from the recipes in this book, substitute your favorite fresh or bottled tomato salsa or hot chili sauce, along with slices of firm but ripe Hass avocado.
* To save yourself postcooking kitchen time, simply cut the steak into the number of portions you're serving, provide guests with sharp steak knives, and let them cut up the meat and vegetables to their own liking.
* For further embellishments, offer Cantina Scallions (page 140), shredded lettuce, shredded Cheddar or Jack cheese, and chopped fresh cilantro.

pizzaiola
burgers

This quick, casual recipe endows beef burgers with the flavors of a great pizza.

— 4 servings —

2 garlic cloves, peeled and cut in halves

4 fresh basil leaves

1½ pounds good-quality ground beef

½ cup grated Parmesan cheese

2 tablespoons tomato paste

1 tablespoon dried oregano

1 teaspoon sugar

4 soft good-quality sandwich rolls or burger buns, split

2 tablespoons extra-virgin olive oil

Preheat the grill.

Meanwhile, prepare the burger mixture. Turn on a food processor fitted with metal blades and drop three of the garlic clove halves and the basil leaves through the feed tube to chop them finely. Stop the machine, scrape down the sides of the work bowl, and add the ground beef, Parmesan, tomato paste, oregano, and sugar. Pulse the machine on and off several times until the ingredients are well mixed. With clean hands, form the mixture into four equal circular patties about ¾ inch thick. Set the patties aside on a plate. Wash your hands and then brush the cut sides of the rolls with the olive oil.

Carefully oil the grill rack. Put the burgers on the grill and cook until done medium well, 12 to 14 minutes, turning once. During the last 2 minutes or so, put the roll halves oiled sides down on the grill to toast until golden.

Quickly rub the toasted side of each roll half lightly with the cut side of the remaining garlic clove half. Place a burger on the bottom half of each roll and serve with condiments for guests to add to taste.

quick tips & variations

* If you like, top the burgers with sliced or shredded mozzarella cheese about 2 minutes before they're done.
* Shredded fresh basil leaves make a fine addition to the meat mixture.
* Sliced sun-ripened tomatoes would go very well with these burgers.

smoky ham-and-cheese beef burgers

Here's a natural for people who love bacon on their cheeseburgers. In this case, smoky ham is blended with the beef to extend its flavor throughout, and even more aromatic richness is gained by topping the jumbo burgers with smoked Cheddar cheese.

———————————— 4 servings —

1¼ pounds extra-lean ground beef

¼ pound honey-glazed smoked ham, finely chopped

¼ pound smoked Cheddar cheese, cut into thin slices

4 burger buns

2 tablespoons unsalted butter, melted

2 tablespoons honey mustard (optional)

Preheat the grill.

Meanwhile, prepare the burgers. Put the ground beef and chopped ham in a mixing bowl. With clean hands, thoroughly mix the beef and ham. Form the mixture into four equal patties about ¾ inch thick, setting them aside on a plate. Wash your hands. Brush the cut sides of the burger buns with the melted butter, setting them on a separate plate.

Carefully oil the grill rack. Put the burgers on the grill and cook them until done medium well, 12 to 14 minutes, turning once. About 2 minutes before they're done, place the cheese slices on top of them. Put the buns cut sides down on the grill to toast just until golden. Place the burgers on the toasted buns and, if you like, serve with honey mustard.

quicktips &variations

* Prepackaged, sliced cooked ham of any kind works well for this recipe.
* Feel free to substitute smoked mozzarella or provolone for the Cheddar, or use a good, mild-to-sharp nonsmoked Cheddar.
* A honey mustard works well with the flavors in this recipe. If you don't have a jar of honey-flavored mustard, you can make your own by mixing three parts Dijon or brown mustard with one part honey. Or use another mustard or condiment of your choice.

chipotle-orange veal chops

Chipotle chilies, the smoke-dried form of spicy jalapeños, add aromatic flavor and a touch of fire to grilled veal. A splash of orange echoes the sweetness in both the chilies and the meat.

— 4 servings

4 1-to-1½-inch-thick bone-in veal chops (about 12 ounces each)

3 or 4 chipotle chilies in adobo sauce

¼ cup orange juice

2 tablespoons grated orange zest

2 tablespoons light or dark brown sugar

Salt

Black pepper

Preheat the grill.

Meanwhile, prepare the chops. Trim excess fat from the veal chops and set them aside, placing them side by side in a shallow dish at room temperature. In a small bowl, mash the chipotle chilies and add 2 tablespoons of the adobo sauce in which they were canned. Stir in the orange juice and sugar. Smear half of the sauce evenly over both sides of the veal chops, reserving the remainder for basting.

Carefully oil the grill rack. Season the chops with salt and black pepper to taste. Place them on the grill rack and cook, turning once, and baste several times with the reserved sauce until done to your liking, 18 to 20 minutes for medium.

quick tips & variations

* This also works well with boneless veal steaks and with beefsteaks.
* If the veal chops are particularly thick, you might want to try injecting about a third of the chipotle mixture sideways into the meat using a meat syringe (page 12). Then, smear another third of the mixture on the outside of the chops and reserve the remaining third for basting.
* Fire-Licked Guacamole (page 161) makes a great accompaniment.

veal pockets with smoked mozzarella and anchovy

The inspiration for this dish comes from *vitello tonnato*, an Italian specialty of cold sliced veal dressed with a rich sauce of mayonnaise, tuna, and anchovies. The surprisingly good combination of briny and mellow, sweet flavors translates well to the grill for a special-occasion main course.

— 4 servings —

Preheat the grill. Soak 12 long, wooden cocktail picks in a bowl of cold water.

Meanwhile, prepare the veal. One at a time, place the cutlets between two sheets of waxed paper and pound them with a meat pounder or rolling pin to flatten them to a uniform thickness of about 1/3 inch. In a mixing bowl or large, shallow dish, stir together the oil and lemon juice. Add the veal cutlets and turn them in the mixture to coat them well. One at a time, smear 1/2 teaspoon of anchovy paste on one side of each veal cutlet. Arrange sliced smoked mozzarella on top, folding in the cheese to leave a margin at the wider end of the cutlet. Sprinkle the cheese with the parsley. Fold each cutlet in half, bringing the narrower side over the wider side. Tuck the sides over to enclose the filling. Secure each of the three open sides by passing a long, wooden cocktail pick down through both halves, along the underside, and back up. Leave the veal in the oil-lemon mixture to marinate.

Carefully oil the grill rack. Season the veal with salt and black pepper to taste, place it on the grill, and cook, turning several times, until well browned and cooked through, about 20 minutes total. Transfer the veal to a platter or individual serving plates and, using a kitchen towel or paper towels to protect your fingers, pull out the cocktail picks before serving the veal with lemon wedges.

4 **veal top round cutlets (1¼ to 1½ pounds total weight)**

2 **tablespoons extra-virgin olive oil**

1 **tablespoon lemon juice**

2 **teaspoons anchovy paste**

2 **ounces smoked mozzarella cheese, thinly sliced**

1 **tablespoon chopped fresh Italian parsley**

Salt

Black pepper

1 **lemon, cut into wedges**

quick tips & variations

* Tubes of anchovy paste are sold near the canned anchovies in well-stocked markets. Or use good-quality anchovy fillets and mash them yourself.
* Substitute plain mozzarella or provolone for the smoked mozzarella.
* Replace the anchovy paste with 1 teaspoon good-quality pesto.
* For simpler assembly, follow the procedure described in the recipe for Chicken Breasts Napolitano (page 86).
* This recipe also works well with chicken.

pork chops with maple-cider glaze

The sweet, earthy flavors of maple syrup and apple cider are natural partners for good-quality pork.

— 4 servings —

2 tablespoons unsalted butter

2 tablespoons finely minced shallots or onions

¼ cup apple cider vinegar

6 tablespoons pure maple syrup

4 1-to-1½-inch bone-in, center-cut pork loin chops (about ½ pound each)

Salt

Black pepper

Preheat the grill.

Meanwhile, prepare the glaze. In a small saucepan over medium heat, melt the butter. Add the shallots and sauté until they just begin to soften, about 2 minutes. Add the vinegar, raise the heat to high, and simmer briskly until the cider has reduced to a syrupy glaze that bubbles crisply, 2 to 3 minutes. Remove the pan from the heat, stir in the maple syrup thoroughly, and set aside.

Carefully oil the grill rack. Season the pork chops generously with salt and black pepper to taste, place them on the grill, and spoon a little of the glaze on top of them. Grill the chops until just slightly pink in the center, 12 to 14 minutes total cooking time, turning them several times and continuing to spoon the glaze over them every couple of minutes.

quicktips &variations

* The glaze also works very well with pork tenderloins and with veal.
* For added flavor, spoon a couple of tablespoons of the glaze into a meat syringe and carefully inject the mixture sideways into each pork chop in several places along its meaty edge, keeping the needle tip clear of the bone.
* Accompany with Pie-Spiced Apple Rings with Butter and Brown Sugar (page 164) or Brown Sugar–Crusted Pineapple Rings (page 169), if you like.

mustard-honey glazed pork and dried apricot kebabs

This sweet-spicy combination of flavors goes perfectly with pork.

4 servings

Preheat the grill. If using bamboo or wooden skewers, put them in a bowl of cold water to soak.

While the grill is heating, prepare the pork and apricots. Trim any excess fat from the tenderloin and cut it into 1½-inch cubes. Arrange the pieces in a single layer in a nonreactive baking dish or other container. In a cup or bowl, stir together half of the wine with the salt, sugar, and ginger. When the salt and sugar have dissolved, pour the mixture over the pork cubes and turn once to coat them well. Leave them to soak, turning occasionally, until the fire is ready. Put the remaining wine in a microwave-proof bowl. Add the apricots and heat them in the microwave briefly, just until the wine is hot. Remove the bowl from the microwave and leave the apricots to plump in the wine.

Just before grilling, drain the apricots, reserving the wine in which they soaked. Stir the mustard and honey into this soaking wine and set aside. Thread the pork cubes on skewers, alternating them with the apricots. Discard the pork marinade.

Carefully oil the grill rack. Season the kebabs with salt and black pepper to taste. Place the kebabs on the grill and cook, turning them occasionally and basting with the honey-mustard wine mixture, until the pork is just cooked through, 14 to 16 minutes. Glaze the kebabs with the last of the basting mixture about 1 minute before they are done.

1½ pounds pork tenderloin or other tender, boneless cut of pork

1 cup dry white wine

1 teaspoon salt

1 teaspoon sugar

½ teaspoon ground ginger

16 dried apricots

2 tablespoons Dijon mustard

2 tablespoons honey

quicktips & variations

* Make sure the dimensions of the apricots are not bigger than the pork cubes. The apricots should also be threaded evenly on the skewers, or the fruit may scorch.
* Ask the butcher to trim and cut the pork for you to the desired dimensions. Other tender cuts of boneless pork may be used in place of the tenderloin.
* Substitute ground cardamom or ground coriander for the ginger.

three-chili-glazed pork tenderloin

Three different sources of chili give surprising depth of flavor to this quick pork main course: a rub of mild pure chili powder, a glaze based on sweet-hot pepper jelly, and hot chili sauce, easily injected into the center of the meat with a syringe (see page 12).

— 4 to 6 servings —

2 whole pork tenderloins (1¾ to 2 pounds total weight)

4 tablespoons Sriracha or other chili sauce

6 tablespoons jalapeño jelly or other pepper jelly

3 tablespoons good-quality dry red wine

2 teaspoons mild pure red chili powder

1 teaspoon salt

½ teaspoon black pepper

Preheat the grill for medium-hot cooking.

While the grill is heating, prepare the pork. Trim any excess fat from the tenderloins and put them in a shallow dish. Transfer the chili sauce to a meat syringe. From the thick end of one of the tenderloins, carefully plunge the syringe deep into the center of the meat along its length until the tip reaches the middle. Then, slowly pull out the syringe while slowly pressing down on the plunger to inject about half a tablespoon of the chili sauce along the length of that half of the tenderloin. Repeat from the other end. Then, inject another half tablespoon of the chili sauce in several other evenly spaced places. Repeat this process with the other tenderloin.

In a bowl, stir together the jelly and the wine. Reserve half of the jelly for glazing the pork. Pour the other half into a sauce bowl and set it aside for serving. In another small bowl, stir together the chili powder, salt, and black pepper. Rub the chili powder mixture all over the pork tenderloins.

Carefully oil the grill rack. Place the tenderloins on the grill and cook them, turning occasionally, until evenly well seared all over with grill marks, 5 to 6 minutes total. Move the tenderloins closer to the side of the grill and continue cooking until they are barely pink in the center and register 155°F when a meat thermometer is inserted into its

the kindest cut of pork

Whole tenderloin is one of the best choices you can make when you want to grill pork quickly and artfully. The foot-long cylinder of meat is easy to handle and cooks in a relatively short time. Yet its larger size helps retain moisture well, a genuine boon considering that today's pork has been bred to be leaner, and therefore drier, than in the past. Nonetheless, a properly cooked whole tenderloin will yield juicy slices when you cut it crosswise after it comes off the grill.

Not all meat markets will have whole tenderloins available, and you may have to ask your butcher for it a day or more in advance. Lately, and very encouragingly, vacuum-sealed plastic packages containing two whole tenderloins from a major national pork producer have been showing up in my local supermarket chain. These provide the perfect quantity of tenderloin for 4 to 6 servings.

thickest part, 12 to 15 minutes more, turning the tenderloins halfway through. Then, spoon half of the jelly-wine mixture you've reserved for glazing over the pork's surface. One minute later, turn the tenderloin over and spoon the remaining glaze on top, then turn the tenderloin over again for 1 minute more to finish setting the glaze.

Remove the tenderloins from the heat to a serving platter or cutting board, cover them loosely with foil, and let them rest for 5 minutes. Carve the tenderloins crosswise into ½-inch-thick slices and transfer to serving plates. Drizzle any juices that collected over the pork slices. Pass the sauce bowl with remaining wine-jelly mixture for guests to use as a condiment.

quicktips & variations

* If you can't find pork tenderloins easily, substitute thick pork chops, taking care to keep the tip of the meat syringe clear of any bones.
* Sriracha is a Thai-style, garlic-flavored red chili sauce sold in squeeze bottles in Asian markets, and is increasingly available in the Asian foods section of well-stocked supermarkets. Feel free to substitute any other kind of thick, smooth red chili sauce.
* Pepper jelly made with jalapeños has a good, hot bite, but feel free to substitute another, milder pepper jelly of your choice.
* For a more formal meal, serve the tenderloin and its juices and sauce with potatoes or rice. You can also enjoy it casually in a sandwich made with split burger buns or good-quality bakery rolls.
* Leftovers will be terrific the next day sliced even more thinly for sandwiches, with pepper jelly spooned on straight from the jar as a condiment.

meat

barbecue-basted pork tenderloin

Usually, the flavor of true barbecued pork takes hours of marinating and basting. This recipe achieves similar flavor in next to no time, thanks to a meat syringe and a quickly assembled barbecue sauce.

———— 4 to 6 servings ——

2 whole pork tenderloins
(1¾ to 2 pounds total weight)

2 tablespoons cider vinegar

2 tablespoons dark brown sugar

2 tablespoons tomato paste

1 tablespoon molasses

1 tablespoon corn oil

1 teaspoon mild pure red chili powder

½ teaspoon natural hickory seasoning (Liquid Smoke) (optional)

2 medium garlic cloves, peeled

1 teaspoon salt

½ teaspoon black pepper

Preheat the grill.

Meanwhile, prepare the pork. Trim any excess fat from the tenderloins and put them in a shallow dish.

In a bowl, stir together the vinegar and brown sugar until the sugar dissolves. Stir in the tomato paste, molasses, corn oil, chili powder, and hickory seasoning, if using. Press the garlic cloves through a garlic press and into the bowl. Transfer 4 tablespoons of this sauce to a meat syringe. From each end of each tenderloin, carefully plunge the syringe deep into the center of the meat until the tip reaches halfway along its length. Then, slowly pull out the syringe while slowly pressing down on the plunger to inject the barbecue sauce along the length of that half of the tenderloin. Inject 2 tablespoons total of sauce per tenderloin.

Carefully oil the grill rack. Generously season the tenderloins all over with the salt and black pepper. Place them on the grill and cook, turning them occasionally, until evenly well seared all over with grill marks, 5 to 6 minutes total. Move the tenderloins closer to the side of the grill and baste them with a little of the remaining barbecue sauce. Continue cooking the tenderloins, turning them 3 or 4 times and basting until the tenderloins are barely pink in the center and register 155°F when a meat thermometer is inserted into their thickest part, 12 to 15 minutes more.

Remove the tenderloins from the heat to a serving platter, cover them loosely with foil, and let rest for 5 minutes. Carve the tenderloins crosswise into ½-inch-thick slices and transfer to serving plates. Drizzle the juices that collected in the platter over the pork slices.

* If you can't find pork tenderloins easily, substitute thick pork chops, taking care to keep the tip of the meat syringe clear of any bones.
* You'll find Liquid Smoke in the seasonings section of well-stocked markets. It adds a nice hickory smoke flavor to the sauce, but is not essential.
* For even spicier barbecue, you can double the mild chili powder or substitute pure hot chili powder.
* Serve the sliced pork with rice or potatoes. Or for true casual, country-style barbecue, cut the pork into thinner slices, pile them inside a soft bun or roll, and top with a generous dollop of your favorite cole slaw, either homemade or bought from a supermarket or deli.

jamaican-style jerked pork tenderloin

Scholars debate whether the Jamaican term "jerk" comes from the same Spanish root as "jerky," *charqui,* meaning cooked or cured meat. It might also describe the process of poking meat all over with a skewer (or, for that matter, rubbing it vigorously) to help the seasonings penetrate. No one can contest, however, the powerful impact of traditional hot-spicy-sweet jerk seasonings, translated here into a simple rub made with pantry staples. Serve with Brown Sugar–Crusted Pineapple Rings (page 169).

— 4 to 6 servings —

2 whole pork tenderloins (1¾ to 2 pounds total weight)

2 tablespoons light or dark brown sugar

2 teaspoons salt

2 teaspoons black pepper

2 teaspoons cayenne pepper

2 teaspoons dried basil, crumbled

2 teaspoons dried thyme, crumbled

1 teaspoon sweet paprika

½ teaspoon powdered ginger

½ teaspoon ground cinnamon

⅛ teaspoon ground cloves

¼ cup orange juice

2 tablespoons grated yellow onion

2 tablespoons extra-virgin olive oil

quicktips &variations

* The seasoning proportions given are authentically, pleasantly hot. If you like, use as little as half the amount of cayenne.
* Alternatively, use a commercial blend of jerk seasonings.
* Steamed white rice will help soothe the palate and soak up the delicious juices.

Preheat the grill.

Meanwhile, prepare the pork. Trim any excess fat from the tenderloins and put them in a shallow dish.

In a small bowl, stir together the brown sugar, salt, black pepper, cayenne pepper, basil, thyme, paprika, ginger, cinnamon, and cloves. Add the orange juice and grated onion, then stir to make a loose paste. Rub the tenderloins all over with the olive oil and then with the spice mixture. Leave the tenderloins at room temperature.

Carefully oil the grill rack. Place the tenderloins on the grill and cook, turning them occasionally, until evenly well seared all over with grill marks, 5 to 6 minutes total. Move the tenderloins closer to the side of the grill. Continue cooking the tenderloins, turning them three or four times, until the tenderloins are barely pink in the center and register 155°F when a meat thermometer is inserted into their thickest part, 12 to 15 minutes more.

Remove the tenderloins from the heat to a serving platter, cover them loosely with foil, and let them rest for 5 minutes. Carve the tenderloins crosswise into ½-inch-thick slices and transfer to serving plates. Drizzle the juices that collected in the platter over the pork slices.

italian sausage and pepper skewers with balsamic glaze

Quickly assembled kebabs capture the festive flavors of a favorite specialty at Italian street markets and fairs.

— 4 servings —

Preheat the grill. If using wooden or bamboo skewers, put them in a bowl of cold water to soak.

Meanwhile, prepare the sausages. With a fork, puncture each one two or three times. Put the sausages in a saucepan of cold water. Put the pan over medium-high heat. When the water comes to a full rolling boil, drain the sausages and then rinse them in cold running water until they are cool enough to handle. Cut each sausage crosswise into 1-inch pieces. Put the sausage chunks in a mixing bowl and add the bell pepper and onion pieces. Drizzle the sausage with the olive oil and toss well to coat all the pieces evenly. Thread them onto the skewers, alternating the pieces and passing the skewer through the curved casing sides of each sausage chunk.

Carefully oil the grill rack. Grill the skewers, turning occasionally and basting lightly with the balsamic vinegar, until the sausage chunks are cooked through and they and the vegetables are nicely browned, 8 to 10 minutes.

1½ pounds hot or sweet fresh Italian sausages

1 red or green bell pepper, halved, stemmed, seeded, and cut into 1-inch squares

1 red onion, cut into 1-inch chunks

¼ cup extra-virgin olive oil

¼ cup balsamic vinegar

quick tips & variations

* Choose chili-flecked hot Italian sausages or mild, sweet Italian sausages scented with fennel seed. If you like, substitute similarly seasoned fresh sausages made with turkey or chicken for the pork.
* For a classic presentation, serve the grilled sausage and vegetables over instant polenta mounded on individual serving plates.
* For a more casual presentation, slide the kebabs off their skewers into good-quality hot dog buns or Italian rolls that have been split, brushed with oil, and toasted on the grill. Your favorite mustard makes a good condiment.

bacon-wrapped cheddar dogs

Just a few minutes of simple assembly while the grill heats up turn ordinary hot dogs into artistic creations.

— 4 servings —

4 good-quality plump hot dogs

2 ounces sharp Cheddar cheese, cut into thin strips

4 strips smoked bacon

4 good-quality hot dog buns, split open but not separated

1½ tablespoons unsalted butter, melted

quicktips &variations

* Use your favorite type of hot dog: pork, beef, turkey, or a blend.
* Don't use dogs that are too thick, such as knockwurst, because the bacon wrapping will burn before the sausage is completely heated through.
* If you like, smear a favorite condiment into the slit before stuffing the hot dog with cheese. Dijon mustard or a bright yellow ballpark-style mustard works especially well. A little hot pepper jelly is an eye-opening sweet-hot variation.
* Feel free to vary the type of cheese, using a good melting variety from mild Cheddar to Monterey Jack, Swiss to smoked Gouda.
* Top off the finished dog Chicago-style, piling chopped onion, fresh tomato, and dill pickle spears into the bun.

Preheat the grill for medium-hot cooking. Put 8 sturdy, wooden toothpicks into a bowl of cold water to soak for a few minutes.

Prepare the hot dogs. With the tip of a small, sharp knife, make a slit along the hot dog's entire length, cutting down about two-thirds of the way through its diameter. Evenly place the cheese strips inside the slit in each hot dog. Drape the end of a bacon strip over the slit at one end of the stuffed hot dog; with the bacon at a 45-degree angle to the hotdog, carefully wrap the bacon in a spiral around the dog. Secure the end of the bacon at each end of the hot dog by passing one of the soaked toothpicks through both the bacon and the hot dog. Brush the split interiors of each bun with the melted butter.

Carefully oil the grill rack. Place the hot dogs on the grill rack and cook, turning once with tongs, until the bacon is evenly browned and crisp, 6 to 8 minutes total. Take care not to overcook or burn the bacon. For the last 2 minutes or so, carefully place the split hot dog buns buttered sides down on the grill to toast just until golden. With the tongs, place a hot dog in each bun. Shield your fingertips with a kitchen towel or paper towel and pull out the toothpicks from the ends of each dog.

grilled ham steaks with spicy pineapple glaze and provolone

These are ideal for a luau-style cookout. Being pre-cooked, the ham steaks take just a few minutes to prepare and come out perfectly glazed in the time it takes to heat them through.

— 4 servings —

Preheat the grill.

Meanwhile, prepare the ham steaks. Place them in a shallow dish large enough to hold them side by side. In a small bowl, stir together the pineapple jam and chili sesame oil. Smear the mixture evenly over both sides of the ham steaks.

Carefully oil the grill rack. Place the ham steaks on the grill and cook until their undersides are seared, 1½ to 2 minutes. Turn them over, immediately top them with the provolone, and grill 1½ to 2 minutes more.

4 thick slices precooked smoked ham (about 1 pound total)

3 tablespoons pineapple jam

½ teaspoon Asian hot chili sesame oil

4 thin slices provolone cheese (about 1 ounce each)

quicktips & variations

* If you can't find a good-service deli to cut the ham for you, substitute good-quality presliced, packaged ham from the refrigerated case. As long as the thin slices are neatly and compactly stacked, you can keep several of them stuck together to compose the 4 thicker slices called for.
* If you can't find hot chili sesame oil, substitute regular toasted sesame oil and a good dash of hot pepper sauce.
* To add a spicy herbaceous note, mix a tablespoon or two of chopped fresh cilantro leaves with the jam and oil.
* The ham is wonderful served as a sandwich between slices of sourdough bread that have been brushed with butter and toasted on the grill.

mint-soy lamb chops

Europe and Asia meet in a sophisticated yet simple flavor combination that adds extra savor to lamb.

— 4 servings —

4 ¾-inch-thick boneless lamb chops (about 1½ pounds total)

¼ cup mint jelly, plus more as a condiment

1½ tablespoons soy sauce

2 teaspoons vegetable oil

Black pepper

Fresh mint sprigs, for garnish (optional)

Preheat the grill.

Meanwhile, prepare the lamb chops. Trim them of any fat or connective tissue. In a small bowl, stir together the mint jelly, soy sauce, and vegetable oil. Spoon about 1 tablespoon of the mixture over the lamb chops, turning to coat them with it. Leave at room temperature and reserve the remaining mint-soy mixture.

When the grill is ready, season the lamb chops with black pepper to taste. Carefully oil the grill rack. Place the chops on the grill. Cook, basting with the remaining mint-soy mixture and turning once, until done to your liking, 13 to 15 minutes for medium. Transfer to individual serving plates, garnish with mint sprigs if desired, and pass around extra mint jelly for guests to use as a condiment.

quicktips &variations

* For a more tangy, complex flavor, seek out an English or Irish brand of mint jelly that includes vinegar. Sweeter American-made mint jellies will work fine, however.
* The lamb will cook more quickly, and absorb more flavor, if you flatten it slightly using a meat pounder before coating it with the mint-soy mixture.
* This recipe also works well with bone-in lamb chops and other forms of grilled lamb.
* Serve the lamb chops atop steamed sticky Asian-style rice to absorb their juices.

rosemary-lemon-garlic lamb chops

The combination of seasonings could place this eloquently simple recipe just about anywhere along the Mediterranean's sunny northern shore.

— 4 servings —

Preheat the grill.

Meanwhile, prepare the lamb chops. Trim the chops of any excess fat or connective tissue and place them in a shallow dish large enough to hold them in a single layer. In a mixing bowl, combine the olive oil, rosemary, lemon juice, and lemon zest. Press the garlic through a garlic press and into the bowl, then stir to combine. Smear the mixture all over both sides of the lamb chops and leave them at room temperature.

Carefully oil the grill rack. Season the lamb chops generously with salt and black pepper to taste. Cook until done to your liking, 13 to 15 minutes for medium. Transfer to individual serving plates and garnish with lemon wedges and, if available, individual little sprigs of fresh rosemary.

4 1-inch-thick lamb chops (about 1½ pounds total)

2 tablespoons extra-virgin olive oil

1 tablespoon finely minced fresh rosemary leaves, or 2 tablespoons crumbled dried rosemary

1 tablespoon lemon juice

1 tablespoon grated lemon zest

2 garlic cloves, peeled

   Salt

   Black pepper

1 lemon, cut into wedges

   Fresh rosemary sprigs for garnish (optional)

quick tips & variations

* This recipe also works well with boneless lamb chops or with other forms of grilled lamb.
* For an especially elegant presentation, look for tiny Frenched baby lamb rib chops. For 4 servings, buy a dozen of them, a total weight of 1½ to 2 pounds.

greek lamb chops with feta and kalamata olive salsa

A medley of bold, tangy Mediterranean flavors highlight the rich, sweet flavor of lamb.

4 servings

feta and kalamata olive salsa

2 large, firm, ripe Roma tomatoes, cored, halved, seeded, and cut into ¼-inch cubes (about 1¼ cups)

½ cup crumbled feta cheese (about 2 ounces)

½ cup coarsely chopped, pitted Kalamata olives

½ cup finely chopped fresh Italian parsley

2 tablespoons extra-virgin olive oil

1 tablespoon lemon juice

¼ teaspoon salt

Black pepper

greek lamb chops

4 1-inch thick lamb chops (about 1½ pounds total)

2 tablespoons extra-virgin olive oil

1½ tablespoons finely chopped fresh oregano leaves, or 1 tablespoon crumbled dried oregano

1 tablespoon lemon juice

Salt

Black pepper

Preheat the grill.

Meanwhile, make the salsa and prepare the lamb chops. For the salsa, in a mixing bowl stir together the tomatoes, feta cheese, olives, parsley, olive oil, lemon juice, salt, and black pepper. Cover with plastic wrap and refrigerate.

To prepare the lamb chops, trim any excess fat or connective tissue from the chops. In a shallow dish or bowl large enough to hold the chops side by side, stir together the olive oil, fresh or dried oregano, and lemon juice. Add the chops and turn them in the mixture to coat them thoroughly. Set aside at room temperature.

When the grill is ready, season the lamb chops with salt and black pepper to taste. Carefully oil the grill rack. Place the chops on the grill. Cook until done to your liking, 13 to 15 minutes for medium. Transfer to individual serving plates and heap the Feta and Kalamata Olive Salsa over or alongside the chops.

quick tips
& variations

* This recipe also works well with boneless lamb chops or other forms of grilled lamb.
* Many markets sell packages of already crumbled feta cheese.
* Look for jars of already pitted Kalamata olives in the pickle section of well-stocked markets. For a less assertive flavor, substitute canned pitted black California olives.
* If you like, add a little fresh or dried oregano to the salsa.
* Try this salsa with other grilled meats, poultry, or seafood.

lamb chop choices

Lamb is one of my favorite meats for quick, artistic grilling. The searing heat and hint of smoke show off its sweet, delicately gamy flavor to outstanding advantage.

Relatively young and tender as the meat is, many different cuts work well for grilling, including the boneless leg of lamb called for in the Tandoori-Style Leg of Lamb with Vegetable-Herb Raita, page 80. But lamb chops are among the quickest and most attractive of lamb choices. Chops, characterized by one or more bones extending from a disc of meat, come from more than one part of the animal, and may range in size from tiny single-bone rib chops offering barely more than a bite apiece to robust, single-serving loin chops.

tandoori-style leg of lamb

with vegetable-herb raita

Put together in just a minute or so, a yogurt-and-spice paste transforms lamb into a classic Indian dish. Accompanying it, the raita, a yogurt-and-vegetable salad, offers a refreshing counterpoint with every bite.

— 6 servings —

vegetable-herb raita

- 1 cup plain yogurt
- 1 firm, ripe Roma tomato, cored, halved, seeded, and cut into ¼-inch cubes (about ½ cup)
- 1 pickling cucumber, coarsely shredded (about ½ cup)
- ½ red bell pepper, cored, seeded, and cut into ¼-inch cubes (about ½ cup)
- ¼ red onion, finely chopped (about ½ cup)
- 1 tablespoon coarsely chopped fresh mint leaves
- 1 tablespoon coarsely chopped fresh cilantro leaves
- 1 tablespoon lemon juice
- ¼ teaspoon salt

tandoori-style leg of lamb

- 2½ pounds boneless leg of lamb
- 3 tablespoons plain yogurt
- 1 tablespoon grated fresh ginger root
- 1 teaspoon sweet paprika
- ½ teaspoon cayenne pepper
- ½ teaspoon ground cumin
- ½ teaspoon ground coriander
- ½ teaspoon sugar
- 2 medium garlic cloves, peeled
  Salt
  Black pepper

Preheat the grill.

Meanwhile, prepare the Vegetable-Herb Raita and the lamb. For the raita, put the yogurt in a mixing bowl, reserving 3 tablespoons in a separate large bowl for the lamb. Add the tomato, cucumber, bell pepper, onion, mint, cilantro, lemon juice, and salt. Cover with plastic wrap and refrigerate.

For the lamb, first trim any surface fat or connective tissue from the leg of lamb. To the 3 tablespoons yogurt in the bowl, add the ginger, paprika, cayenne, cumin, coriander, and sugar. Press the garlic cloves through a garlic press and into the bowl, stirring well to make a paste. Add the lamb to the bowl and smear the paste all over the lamb's surface. Set aside.

Carefully oil the grill rack. Season the lamb all over with salt and black pepper to taste and put it on the grill. Cook it until evenly well seared all over with grill marks, about 3 minutes per side. Move it closer to the side of the grill and continue cooking until the lamb is done to your liking, about 25 minutes for medium. A meat thermometer inserted into the thickest part should measure 135°F. Remove the lamb to a platter, cover it with aluminum foil, and let it rest for 5 minutes before carving across the grain into slices about ¼ inch thick. Serve, passing the Vegetable-Herb Raita for guests to add to their plates to taste.

quick tips
& variations

* Ask your butcher to bone and butterfly the leg of lamb for you. You'll be grilling it in a large, flat piece rather than rolled and tied as some butchers sell it. If the meat has some particularly large lobes, you can ensure more even cooking by butterflying the thicker portions with a small, sharp knife, cutting them horizontally in half and leaving them connected at the meat's outer edge.

* This recipe also works well with lamb tenderloins and chops, diminishing the cooking time according to the size of the individual cuts.

* Pickling cucumbers are the 4-to-6-inch-long kind used to make deli-style dill pickles. You'll find them fresh in the produce section of well-stocked markets. If you can't find one, substitute a comparably sized section of a seedless English cucumber.

* If you like, accompany with Naan-Style Garlic Butter Pita (page 39) and Curry-Dusted Acorn Squash Crescents (page 157).

middle eastern minced lamb kebabs
with tzatziki and mint-onion relish

Although the aromatic ground lamb mixture is tradition- ally molded and cooked on skewers, you don't really need to fuss with them to make this flavorful dish. The two accompaniments—a fragrant yogurt sauce and a simple relish—make the dish especially impressive.

4 servings

tzatziki

1 cup plain yogurt

2 garlic cloves, peeled

½ teaspoon salt

¼ teaspoon ground cayenne pepper

mint-onion relish

½ yellow onion, finely chopped

¼ cup finely chopped fresh mint leaves

¼ teaspoon salt

lamb kebabs

1½ pounds ground lamb

2 garlic cloves, peeled

1 tablespoon grated onion

1 tablespoon finely chopped fresh Italian parsley

1 tablespoon extra-virgin olive oil

1 teaspoon salt

½ teaspoon ground black pepper

¼ teaspoon ground cayenne pepper

¼ teaspoon ground cumin

1 lemon, cut into 4 wedges

Preheat the grill.

Meanwhile, make the Tzatziki, the Mint-Onion Relish, and the lamb mixture. For the Tzatziki, put the yogurt in a bowl. Press the garlic cloves through a garlic press and into the bowl. Add the salt and cayenne pepper and stir well. Cover with plastic wrap and refrigerate. For the relish, toss together the onion, mint leaves, and salt in a bowl. Cover and refrigerate.

For the lamb, put the ground lamb in a mixing bowl. Press the garlic cloves through a garlic press and into the bowl and add the onion, parsley, olive oil, salt, black pepper, cayenne pepper, and cumin. With clean hands, mix the lamb and seasonings together thoroughly. Cover with plastic wrap and refrigerate.

Carefully oil the grill rack. With clean hands, form the lamb mixture into four long, even sausage shapes resembling plump hot dogs about 8 inches long and about 1½ inches in diameter. Place them perpendicular to the bars of the grill rack and cook, turning occasionally, until evenly browned and done to your liking, 13 to 15 minutes for medium. Transfer to serving plates and pass the Tzatziki, the Mint-Onion Relish, and the lemon wedges for guests to add to their portions to taste.

quick tips & variations

* Many well-stocked supermarkets and butcher shops offer packages of ground lamb. If it is unavailable, ask the butcher to grind some fresh for you from well-trimmed, lean stewing meat or boneless leg of lamb. Or bring the meat home, trim it well, and cut it into 1-inch cubes. Then, firm it up in the freezer for about 30 minutes. Remove the lamb from the freezer and chop it in a food processor with the metal blade, pulsing the machine on and off until the meat is uniformly but not too finely chopped.
* If you like, you can use low-fat or nonfat yogurt for the Tzatziki, but the richer flavor of whole-milk yogurt is most complementary to the lamb mixture.
* Try the Tzatziki and Mint-Onion Relish with other grilled lamb dishes.
* For a casual change of pace, brush the cut surfaces of hot dog buns with a little olive oil and toast them on the grill during the last minute or two of the lamb's grilling time. Serve the kebabs in the buns, using the Tzatziki and relish as you would hot dog condiments.

mongolian lamb

4 boneless lamb steaks (about 1½ pounds total weight)

2 tablespoons soy sauce

1 tablespoon lemon juice

1 tablespoon sugar

½ tablespoon grated fresh ginger

2 garlic cloves, peeled

2 teaspoons Asian hot chili sesame oil

Black pepper

1 lemon, cut into 4 wedges

Lamb is a very popular meat for Mongolian-style barbecue, whose robust Asian flavors are captured here.

————— 4 servings —————

quick tips & variations

* If you can't find hot chili sesame oil, substitute regular Asian toasted sesame oil and add a dash of your favorite hot chili sauce.
* Serve the lamb with steamed rice to soak up its juices.
* Alternatively, serve the lamb with a platter of large, whole lettuce leaves and bowls of shredded carrots, fresh cilantro sprigs, and bean sprouts that you've wilted slightly by putting them in a strainer and pouring boiling water over them. Encourage guests to cut thin strips of the lamb and eat them taco-style, folded inside a lettuce leaf with the other vegetables and a squeeze of lemon.

Carefully oil the grill rack.

Meanwhile, prepare the lamb. Trim the edges of the lamb steaks of any excess fat or connective tissue. One at a time, put the lamb steaks between two sheets of waxed paper and, with a meat pounder or a rolling pin, pound them to a uniform thickness of ¼ to ⅓ inch. In a mixing bowl, stir together the soy sauce, lemon juice, sugar, and ginger. Press the garlic clove through a garlic press and into the bowl, then stir until the sugar has dissolved. Stir in the oil. Pour half of the mixture into another bowl or cup to reserve for basting. Add the lamb to the mixing bowl and turn it to coat it well.

Carefully oil the grill rack. Remove the lamb from the marinade, shaking off the excess and discarding the marinade. Season the lamb generously with black pepper to taste. Place the lamb on the grill and cook, turning once and basting with the reserved soy mixture, until the lamb is cooked through and nicely browned, 4 to 6 minutes total cooking time. Serve immediately with the lemon wedges.

poultry

Not so long ago, grill enthusiasts who felt in need of a creative change of pace turned to poultry—and especially chicken. They'd slather bone-in, skin-on chicken breasts, thighs, wings, and drumsticks with barbecue sauce, toss them on the grill, daub them regularly with more sauce, and in 30 minutes or so, when the chicken had finally cooked through, proudly serve up a platter of blackened, hard chicken briquettes.

The recipes in this chapter produce food that in no way resembles briquettes, but instead tender, moist, flavorful, and attractive poultry main courses. They achieve such tempting results by taking advantage of one of the greatest time-saving boons available to shoppers today in supermarket butcher departments everywhere: ready-to-buy bone-less, skinless cuts of chicken and turkey.

So much poultry is sold without skin today because health-conscious people want nothing to do with all the fat, cholesterol, and calories it contains. Bones are taken out to make the poultry easier to cut up and eat—and to avoid their unsightliness on the plate at the end of the meal. But the elimination of both skin and bones also makes poultry cook far more quickly, and allows a cook to apply creative flavors more directly to the meat itself—the very essence of Quick Grill Artistry.

To make the cooking of boneless, skinless chicken breasts go even faster, flatten them to a uniform thickness of $1/2$ inch by placing them, one at a time, between two sheets of waxed paper and pounding them. This will take 4 to 5 minutes off the total cooking time.

You'll find boneless, skinless chicken thighs prepackaged in the meat section of most supermarkets. Depending on how they were boned, some of the thighs may be uneven in thickness. For quick, even cooking, you can flatten any especially thick lobes of meat with a meat mallet or pounder. You can also butterfly the thicker portions with a small, sharp knife, cutting them horizontally in half and leaving them connected at the edges.

chicken breasts napolitano

In minutes, you can transform boneless, skinless chicken breasts into a trattoria classic.

— 4 servings —

4 boneless skinless chicken breast halves (about 1½ pounds total weight)

2 garlic cloves, peeled

4 tablespoons tomato paste

2 tablespoons freshly grated Parmesan cheese

2 teaspoons dried oregano, crumbled

2 teaspoons sugar

Salt

Black pepper

8 large, whole fresh basil leaves

2 ounces shredded mozzarella cheese

Preheat the grill.

Meanwhile, prepare the chicken breasts and their topping. Trim any fat or connective tissue from them. Place each breast half, one at a time, in between two sheets of waxed paper. With a meat pounder or a rolling pin, pound the chicken breast until it is flattened to a uniform thickness of about ½ inch. For the topping, press the garlic cloves through a garlic press and into a small bowl. Stir in the tomato paste, Parmesan, oregano, and sugar, then set aside.

When the grill is ready, season the chicken breasts generously with salt and black pepper to taste. Carefully oil the grill rack. Place the chicken on the grill rack and cook, turning once, until cooked through, 8 to 10 minutes. About 2 minutes before the chicken breasts are done, smear some of the tomato-and-Parmesan mixture on top of each one and top each with two basil leaves and some of the mozzarella. When the mozzarella has melted, remove the chicken from the grill to a platter or individual serving plates.

quick tips & variations

* Substitute boneless, skinless chicken thighs or turkey cutlets for the chicken.
* The recipe also works well with thin steaks or veal.
* For a spicier version, add about 1/2 teaspoon of crushed red chili flakes to the tomato-and-Parmesan mixture.

chicken breasts with fines herbes butter

A classic French fresh-herb combination adds a delicate flavor profile to grilled chicken breasts.

4 servings

Preheat the grill. Trim any fat or connective tissue from the chicken breasts.

While the grill is heating, make the seasoned butter. In a small bowl, using a fork, mash together the butter and herbs. Set aside.

When the grill is ready, season the chicken breasts generously with salt and white pepper to taste. Carefully oil the grill rack. Place the chicken on the grill rack and cook, turning once, until cooked through, 12 to 14 minutes. Transfer the chicken to serving plates and immediately top each with a dollop of the butter. Garnish with the lemon wedges for guests to squeeze over their servings to taste.

4 boneless, skinless chicken breast halves (about 1½ pounds total weight)

4 tablespoons unsalted butter, softened

4 teaspoons finely chopped fresh basil

4 teaspoons finely chopped fresh chives

4 teaspoons finely chopped fresh dill

4 teaspoons finely chopped fresh parsley

Salt

White pepper

1 lemon, cut into wedges

quicktips &variations

* The seasoned butter is also excellent with firm, white fish such as cod, sea bass, or snapper.
* If you like, add a teaspoonful of Dijon mustard to the butter; or add the grated zest of the lemon.

chicken breasts with sesame-soy-ginger butter

A pat of swiftly seasoned butter forms an instant Asian-style sauce for hot-off-the-grill chicken.

— 4 servings —

4 boneless, skinless chicken breast halves (about 1½ pounds total weight)

4 tablespoons unsalted butter, softened

1 tablespoon finely grated fresh ginger

1 tablespoon soy sauce

1 tablespoon Asian toasted sesame oil

Salt

Black pepper

1 tablespoon toasted sesame seeds

Preheat the grill. Trim any fat or connective tissue from the chicken breasts.

While the grill is heating, make the seasoned butter. In a small bowl, using a fork, mash together the butter, ginger, soy sauce, and sesame oil. Set aside.

When the grill is ready, season the chicken breasts generously with salt and black pepper to taste. Carefully oil the grill rack. Place the chicken on the grill rack and cook, turning once, until cooked through, 12 to 14 minutes. Transfer the chicken to serving plates and immediately top each with a dollop of the butter. Garnish with the toasted sesame seeds.

quick tips & variations

* The butter is also excellent with grilled lamb, pork, or rich-tasting seafood such as salmon or tuna.
* For an edge of vinegary sweetness, substitute finely chopped pink pickled ginger for the fresh ginger. Pickled ginger is the kind served with sushi.
* If you like, add some minced fresh chives or cilantro to the butter.
* Serve with steamed rice and Japanese Cucumbers (see the Salmon Burgers Teriyaki recipe on page 118).

spicy buttermilk chicken breasts

It was my son, Jake's, idea to try to reproduce our favorite oven-fried chicken for the grill. While a floury breading wouldn't work, I felt that the other ingredients we use would translate well. And they do, producing a spicy, down-home flavor.

4 servings

Preheat the grill. Trim any fat or connective tissue from the chicken breasts.

While the grill is heating, stir together the buttermilk and shallots in a mixing bowl large enough to hold the chicken breasts. Add the chicken breasts and turn each one to coat them well.

Just before cooking, stir together the paprika, thyme, sugar, salt, and black pepper. Spread the mixture on a plate. One at a time, remove the chicken breasts from the buttermilk, shake off the excess liquid, and turn each one in the seasoning mixture to coat them.

Carefully oil the grill rack. Place the chicken on the grill rack and cook, turning once, until cooked through, 12 to 14 minutes. Garnish with the lemon wedges for guests to squeeze over their servings to taste.

4 boneless, skinless chicken breast halves (about 1½ pounds total weight)

1 cup cultured 2 percent buttermilk

1 tablespoon grated shallots or onions

1 tablespoon hot paprika

1 teaspoon dried thyme, crumbled

1 teaspoon sugar

1 teaspoon salt

1 teaspoon ground black pepper

1 lemon, cut into wedges

quick tips & variations

* For less spicy but no less flavorful results, use mild, sweet paprika in place of the hot variety.

three-citrus chicken breast fajitas

Latino cooks know well the zesty flavors that result from marinating chicken in a mixture of citrus juices before grilling. This recipe transforms the chicken and its accompanying vegetables into popular fajitas, to be wrapped and eaten in warm tortillas.

—— 4 servings ——

1½ pounds boneless skinless chicken breasts

2 tablespoons lemon juice

2 tablespoons lime juice

2 tablespoons orange juice

3 tablespoons extra-virgin olive oil

1 garlic clove, peeled

1 red bell pepper, quartered, stemmed, and seeded

1 green bell pepper, quartered, stemmed, and seeded

1 sweet yellow or red onion, peeled, trimmed, and cut into 4 slices

Salt

Black pepper

1 lime or lemon, cut into wedges

12 corn tortillas

½ cup coarsely chopped fresh cilantro leaves

Preheat the grill.

Meanwhile, prepare the chicken and vegetables. Trim the chicken breasts. One at a time, place the chicken breasts between two sheets of waxed paper and pound them with a meat pounder or rolling pin to flatten them to a uniform thickness of about ½ inch. In a mixing bowl or large shallow dish, stir together the citrus juices and 1 tablespoon of the oil. Press the garlic clove through a garlic press and stir to combine. Add the flattened chicken breasts and turn them in the mixture to coat them evenly. Put the red and green bell peppers on a plate. Secure the rings of each onion slice by pushing two or three wooden toothpicks through the slice from its side. Add the onions to the peppers, then rub the vegetables evenly with the remaining olive oil.

Carefully oil the grill rack. Lightly season the onions and bell pepper slices with salt and pepper and put them on the grill. About 2 minutes later, remove the chicken breasts from the marinade, shake off any excess liquid, season with salt and black pepper to taste, and put them on the grill. Grill the chicken and vegetables about 8 minutes more, turning them once, until the chicken is cooked through and the vegetables are golden brown. Remove the chicken breasts from the grill to a clean heatproof serving dish and cover them with aluminum foil to keep warm. Distribute the tortillas on the grill and cook them until heated and tender, about 1 minute per side. Stack and wrap them in foil.

To serve the fajitas, quickly but carefully cut the chicken and peppers crosswise into ½-inch-wide strips. Remove the toothpicks from the onion slices and cut the onions in quarters. Return them to the serving dish and toss together. Pass the tortillas and the bowl of fajitas for guests to assemble their own soft tacos. Also, pass the cilantro and lemon or lime wedges in separate bowls for everyone to season their own fajitas.

quick tips & variations

* Packaged chicken tenders may be used in place of chicken breasts. They require no flattening.
* Fire-Licked Guacamole (page 161) is an excellent accompaniment. Alternatively, offer slices of firm but ripe Hass avocado over which you've squeezed a little lime juice.
* Pass your favorite hot pepper sauce, or offer Fire-Roasted Chili-Tomato Salsa (page 162).
* Add two firm, ripe Roma tomatoes to the vegetable mixture, cutting them length-wise in halves, rubbing them with some of the olive oil, and sprinkling them with salt and pepper before grilling along with the bell peppers and onions. Cut each half into four to six chunks after grilling.
* If you like, substitute eight large flour tortillas for the corn tortillas so guests can assemble their own burritos.
* Offer beans and rice as accompaniments to the fajitas.

vietnamese grilled chicken breast salad

A bed of salad vegetables and easy-to-prepare rice noodles paired with a tangy Asian marinade create a grilled salad of great distinction, ideal for a light but satisfying warm-weather meal.

— 4 servings —

1½ pounds boneless, skinless chicken breast halves

2 small green chili peppers, stemmed, seeded, and finely minced

2 shallots, finely minced

½ cup sugar

½ cup lime juice

½ cup fish sauce

¾ cup cold water

½ pound dried thin Asian rice noodles

3 cups mixed baby salad greens

1 carrot, peeled and finely shredded

1 Asian-style cucumber, peeled and finely shredded

½ cup finely shredded fresh basil leaves

½ cup finely shredded fresh mint leaves

½ cup coarsely chopped fresh cilantro leaves

1 lime, cut into 4 wedges

Preheat the grill.

Meanwhile, prepare the chicken, sauce, noodles, and salad. For the chicken, trim the breast of any fat or connective tissue. One at a time, place each breast half between two sheets of waxed paper or plastic wrap. With a meat pounder or rolling pin, flatten the chicken to a thickness of about ¼ inch. Place each flattened chicken breast into a shallow baking dish.

For the sauce, in a mixing bowl stir together the chili peppers, shallots, sugar, lime juice, and fish sauce until the sugar has dissolved. Stir in the water. Pour half of the mixture over the chicken, reserving the other half. Turn the chicken to coat it well with the sauce and leave it at room temperature.

For the salad ingredients, put the rice noodles to soak in a large mixing bowl of warm water. Arrange the salad greens on individual serving plates. As soon as the noodles are soft, after just a few minutes, drain them well and arrange them in nests on each plate. Scatter the shredded carrot and shredded cucumber over the rice noodles.

Carefully oil the grill rack. Shake any excess marinade from the chicken, discarding the marinade. Place the flattened chicken breasts on the grill and cook, turning once, until golden brown on both sides, 7 to 8 minutes total.

Remove the chicken breasts to a clean cutting board in the kitchen and, with a large, sharp knife, cut them crosswise into ½-inch-wide strips. Pile the strips on top of each serving. Generously garnish the chicken with the basil, mint, and cilantro, and pass the reserved sauce and the lime wedges for guests to season the salads to taste.

quicktips &variations

* You'll find fish sauce and rice noodles in Asian markets and in the Asian food section of well-stocked supermarkets.
* For a seafood version of this recipe , try it with jumbo shrimp or sea scallops.
* Bagged, prewashed salad green mixes are ideal for this dish.
* If your supermarket has a salad bar, you can cut your prep time by using preshredded carrots and cucumbers. Feel free to substitute other convenient and appealing prepared vegetables.
* For added flavor and crunch, scatter some roasted cashews, peanuts, or slivered almonds over the chicken before adding the herbs.

chicken breasts stuffed with provolone, ham, and sage

An old Italian restaurant classic finds a welcoming spot on the grill.

4 servings

4 boneless, skinless chicken breast halves (about 1½ pounds total weight)

2 tablespoons extra-virgin olive oil

1 tablespoon lemon juice

1 tablespoon finely chopped fresh sage leaves, or ½ tablespoon dried sage, crumbled

4 thin slices provolone cheese

4 thin slices smoked ham

Salt

Black pepper

quick tips & variations

* Substitute other favorite melting cheeses for the provolone.
* Leave out the sage and, before placing the cheese and ham on one side of the chicken breast, smear it with 1 teaspoon of good-quality prepared pesto.
* If you want to forgo stuffing and securing the packets with cocktail picks, simply follow the assembly procedure described in the recipe for Chicken Breasts Napolitano (page 86).
* The recipe also works very well with veal scaloppini.

Preheat the grill. Soak 12 long wooden cocktail picks in a bowl of cold water.

Meanwhile, prepare the chicken breasts. Trim them of any fat or connective tissue. One at a time, place the chicken breasts between two sheets of waxed paper and pound them with a meat pounder or rolling pin to flatten the breasts to a uniform thickness of about ½ inch. In a mixing bowl or large shallow dish, stir together the oil, lemon juice, and sage. Add the chicken breasts and turn them in the mixture to coat them well. One at a time, arrange a cheese slice and a ham slice on one side of a chicken breast, folding in the cheese and ham to leave a margin at the wider end of the breast. Fold the breast in half, bringing the narrower side over the wider side. Tuck the sides over to enclose the filling. Secure each of the three open sides by passing a long, wooden cocktail pick down through both halves, along the underside, and back up. Leave the packets to marinate in the oil-lemon-sage mixture.

Carefully oil the grill rack. Season the chicken packets with salt and black pepper to taste, place them on the grill, and cook, turning several times, until well browned and the chicken is cooked through, about 25 minutes total. Transfer to a platter or individual serving plates and, using a kitchen towel or paper towels to protect your fingers, pull out the cocktail picks before serving.

convenient chicken tenders

A so-called chicken tender is a thin strip of muscle alongside the breast and attached by a thin membrane. Similar in shape to whole pork or lamb tenderloins but no more than an inch thick and a few inches long, chicken tenders may sometimes be found in markets as part of boneless, skinless chicken breast halves. Often as not, however, they are removed during processing to give the breasts a neater appearance.

As a result, chicken tenders today are often sold packaged by themselves. They cook quickly, and are ideal for rolling up into compact little spirals for skewering on kebabs.

One slight drawback of tenders is that each one usually includes an opaque white strip of sinew that runs along its length and turns chewy when cooked. To remove it, put the tender on a cutting board. With the thumb and forefinger of your weaker hand, grasp the end of the sinew that you'll see sticking out of the tender's wider end. With the other hand, hold the edge of a small, sharp knife blade against the sinew, with the blade slanted safely away from your hands. Keeping the blade edge against the sinew, pull firmly on the end you are grasping, gradually stripping it out of the tender.

springtime chicken tender and baby artichoke kebabs

In these fresh-tasting kebabs, the chicken tenders roll up to the same size and cook in the same time as quickly pared baby artichokes.

— 4 servings —

1 lemon, cut into 8 wedges

16 baby artichokes, each 2½ to 3 inches from base to tip

¼ cup extra-virgin olive oil

2 tablespoons lemon juice

1 tablespoon finely chopped fresh dill or ½ tablespoon dried dill

1½ pounds chicken tenders

Salt

Black pepper

Preheat the grill. If using wooden or bamboo skewers, put them in a bowl of cold water to soak.

Meanwhile, prepare the artichokes and chicken tenders. For the artichokes, fill a large mixing bowl with cold water. Squeeze two lemon wedges into the water. Using a small, sharp knife, pare each artichoke. To do so, first, cut off the stem, flush with the base. Next, starting at the base, pull off the leaves until you get about halfway up the artichoke, exposing paler yellow-green flesh beneath. Finally, cut off the top, green half of the artichoke, leaving a whole baby artichoke heart 1 to 1½ inches in diameter. Drop the artichoke heart in the lemon water.

In another bowl, stir together the olive oil, lemon juice, and dill. Working on a cutting board and using a small, sharp knife, carefully cut any white tendons from the chicken tenders, keeping the blade against the tendon as you pull it away from the meat. Add the chicken tenders to the olive oil mixture. Drain the artichokes, pat them dry with paper towels, and then add them to the chicken. Turn the chicken tenders and artichokes in the mixture to coat them well.

Starting at its wider end, roll up each chicken tender into a compact piece 1 to 1½ inches in diameter. Thread it onto a skewer, passing the tip through the narrow end of the tender and all the way through its rolled-up layers to secure its shape. Add an artichoke heart to the skewer, passing the skewer through the center of its top, leafy end and out through the center of its base. Continue alternating pieces in this way until the skewers are filled.

salmon with orange-soy glaze and black pepper *(page 116)*

smoky ham-and-cheese beef burgers *(page 63)*

tangy bacon-wrapped apricot shrimp skewers *(page 110)*

smoked salmon grilled pizza *(page 44)*

three-citrus chicken breast fajitas *(page 90)*

greek lamb chops with feta and kalamata olive salsa *(page 78)*

cuban steaks with garlic-citrus marinade and orange-onion salsa *(page 52)*

s'mores "quesadillas" *(page 171)*

Carefully oil the grill rack. Season the skewers to taste with salt and black pepper. Put the skewers on the grill and cook, turning several times, until the chicken is cooked through and it and the artichokes are uniformly browned, 13 to 15 minutes. Transfer the kebabs to serving plates and serve with the remaining lemon wedges.

quick tips & variations

* Although the preparation of the baby artichokes may sound a bit complicated, it is quick work and doesn't take much more than about a minute per artichoke.
* Use slender skewers and larger-sized baby artichokes. This way, you'll run a lesser risk of splitting the artichokes during skewering.
* Substitute boneless, skinless chicken breasts for the tenders, cutting them into even chunks 1 to $1^{1}/_{2}$ inches across.
* Fresh or dried oregano, fresh parsley, or fresh basil may be substituted for the dill.

japanese chicken thighs with chili-citrus rub

This chicken recipe's complex, full-flavored seasoning rub comes ready to use in the form of the Japanese table condiment *nanami togarashi,* a commercial blend of chili peppers, sesame seeds, dried seaweed, and orange peel sold in small shakers in Asian markets or in the Asian section of well-stocked supermarkets.

— 4 servings —

1½ pounds boneless, skinless chicken thighs

1½ tablespoons toasted Asian sesame oil

1 tablespoon *nanami togarashi* (a Japanese seasoning)

1 scallion, thinly sliced

Salt

Fresh orange and lemon wedges

Preheat the grill.

Meanwhile, prepare the chicken thighs. With a small, sharp knife, trim off excess fat or connective tissue. Put the chicken thighs on a large platter or baking dish. Drizzle them all over with the sesame oil and rub the oil evenly on both sides. Then sprinkle the thighs on both sides with the *nanami togarashi* and press the seasoning firmly onto the meat.

Carefully oil the grill rack. Place the chicken thighs on the grill and cook them until golden brown on both sides, 12 to 14 minutes total.

As soon as the chicken is done, transfer it to a serving platter or individual plates. Scatter with the chopped scallions and garnish each serving with lemon and orange wedges for each person to squeeze over the chicken to taste.

quick tips & variations

* Serve with steamed rice and Japanese Cucumbers (see the Salmon Burgers Teriyaki recipe on page 118). Or pop the chicken thighs into burger buns that you've brushed with Asian sesame oil and then briefly toasted on the grill.

caribbean chicken thighs with molasses, black pepper, and orange glaze

Combining mellow, sweet, tangy, and pungent flavors, the island-inspired seasonings in this recipe go well with the robust flavor of quick-cooking boneless chicken thighs.

——— 4 servings ———

Preheat the grill.

Meanwhile, prepare the chicken thighs. With a small, sharp knife, trim off excess fat or connective tissue. Put the chicken thighs on a large platter or baking dish. In a small bowl, stir together the molasses and orange juice. Drizzle about a third of the molasses mixture over the chicken thighs, then rub it evenly all over them. Reserve the rest of the mixture for glazing. In a small bowl, stir together the black pepper, salt, and allspice, and sprinkle these seasonings evenly on both sides of the chicken.

Carefully oil the grill rack. Place the chicken thighs on the grill and cook them until golden brown on both sides, 12 to 14 minutes total. About 2 minutes before the thighs are done, spoon half of the reserved molasses mixture over them and flip them over again to set the glaze; a minute later, spoon the remainder of the mixture over the thighs and flip them over again to set the glaze until done.

As soon as the chicken is done, transfer it to a serving platter or individual plates. Garnish each serving with a lime wedge for each person to squeeze over the chicken to taste.

1½ **pounds boneless, skinless chicken thighs**

¼ **cup mild-flavored molasses**

¼ **cup orange juice**

2 **teaspoons coarsely ground black pepper**

½ **teaspoon salt**

¼ **teaspoon ground allspice**

Fresh lime wedges

quicktips &variations

* Rather than fiddling with the adjusting screw on your pepper grinder and grinding for what seems like forever to get two teaspoons, pick up a small container of coarsely ground black pepper in your market's spice section. Preground though it is, it'll still pack plenty of punch.
* Substitute orange or lemon wedges for the lime wedges.

sweet and sour thai chicken thighs

Bottled Asian orange or plum sauce forms the basis for a great poultry glaze that combines sweet, sour, and spicy flavors.

— 4 servings —

1½ pounds boneless, skinless chicken thighs

1 yellow onion, trimmed and cut into 4 slices

1 green or red bell pepper, quartered, stemmed, and seeded

1 cup bottled Chinese orange or plum sauce

1 tablespoon grated fresh ginger root

1 tablespoon soy sauce

½ tablespoon Asian hot chili sesame oil

2 scallions, cut crosswise into very thin slices

½ tablespoon toasted or black sesame seeds

Preheat the grill.

Meanwhile, prepare the chicken thighs. With a small, sharp knife, trim off excess fat or connective tissue. Put the chicken thighs on a large platter or in a shallow baking dish. Secure the rings of the onion slices by pushing 2 or 3 wooden toothpicks from the sides to the center. Add the onions and pepper pieces to the chicken. In a bowl, stir together the orange or plum sauce, ginger, soy sauce, and sesame oil. Pour half of the sauce over the chicken and vegetables, turning once to coat them evenly. Reserve the remaining sauce.

Carefully oil the grill rack. Place the chicken thighs on the grill and cook, basting occasionally with the reserved sauce, until they are golden brown on both sides, 12 to 14 minutes total. About 4 minutes after the chicken starts cooking, add the onion slices and pepper quarters to the grill and cook, basting occasionally, until they are browned and tender, 8 to 10 minutes total. Transfer the chicken thighs and vegetables to a platter or individual serving plates and garnish with the scallions and sesame seeds.

quicktips & variations

* Seek out a good-quality bottled Chinese orange or plum sauce, preferably from an Asian market.
* This recipe also works well with chicken breasts and tenders, and with firm, white-fleshed fish such as sea bass, halibut, or escolar.

mexican chicken burgers

Ground chicken breast, healthy though it is, sometimes tastes bland when grilled as burgers. The seasonings in this recipe really liven them up.

4 servings

Preheat the grill.

Meanwhile, prepare the chicken burger mixture. In a mixing bowl, place the ground chicken, corn kernels, onion, chili powder, and cumin. Press the garlic clove through a garlic press and into the bowl; and using clean hands, lightly but thoroughly combine all the ingredients until well blended. Form the mixture into four equal circular patties about ¾ inch thick. Set aside on a plate. Wash your hands. In a small bowl, stir together the Dijon mustard, mayonnaise, and mild green chilies. Set aside. Brush the cut sides of the rolls with the olive oil.

Carefully oil the grill rack. Season the chicken burgers generously on both sides with salt and black pepper to taste. Place the burgers on the grill rack and cook, turning once, until they are well browned and cooked through, 12 to 14 minutes total. During the last 2 minutes or so, put the roll halves cut sides down on the grill to toast until golden.

Place a chicken burger on the bottom half of each roll and top it with 2 or 3 tomato slices. Serve with the green chili mustard for guests to spread on their burgers to taste.

1½ pounds ground chicken breast

1 can (8¾ ounces) whole-kernel sweet corn, drained

1 small sweet onion, minced

2 teaspoons mild pure red chili powder

½ teaspoon ground cumin

1 clove garlic, peeled

1 tablespoon Dijon mustard

1 tablespoon mayonnaise

2 tablespoons minced mild green Ortega chilies, canned

Salt

Black pepper

4 good-quality soft sandwich rolls or burger buns, split

2 tablespoons olive oil

2 Roma tomatoes, sliced

quicktips &variations

* If your market doesn't have ground chicken, substitute ground turkey. Or buy boneless, skinless chicken breasts, trim them well, cut them into 1-inch chunks, and firm them up in the freezer for 30 minutes. Then chop them in a food processor with the metal blade, pulsing until the mixture is evenly chopped but still slightly coarse.
* For especially luscious burgers, top them with slices of Monterey Jack, pepper Jack, or medium-to-sharp Cheddar cheese.
* Add thinly sliced ripe Hass-style avocado.

poultry

101

turkey breast cutlets with pesto butter

One easy way to safeguard against the possible dryness of turkey breast cutlets is to serve them topped with a dollop of fragrant butter. As anyone knows who has ever enjoyed a turkey-and-pesto sandwich from an Italian deli or imaginative sandwich shop, this combination is a winner.

———— 4 servings ————

4   turkey breast cutlets
    (1½ pounds total)

2   tablespoons extra-virgin
    olive oil

4   tablespoons unsalted butter,
    softened

2   tablespoons finely chopped
    fresh basil

1   tablespoon freshly grated
    Parmesan cheese

2   garlic cloves, peeled

    Salt

    Black pepper

Preheat the grill.

Meanwhile, prepare the turkey cutlets and seasoned butter. Put the turkey breast cutlets on a plate or platter and drizzle them with the olive oil, turning the cutlets in the oil to coat them thoroughly. Set aside. For the seasoned butter, put the butter, basil, and Parmesan cheese in a small bowl. Press the garlic cloves through a garlic press and into the bowl, and using a fork, mash together the ingredients. Set aside.

Carefully oil the grill rack. Season the turkey breast slices with salt and black pepper to taste, put them on the grill rack, and cook, turning once or twice, until cooked through, 8 to 10 minutes total. Transfer the turkey to serving plates and top with dollops of the seasoned butter.

quick tips & variations

* The butter also goes well with chicken, steak, and lamb.
* To add one final element of the classic pesto flavor profile, scatter a few toasted pine nuts over each serving after topping the turkey cutlets with the butter.

turkey breast cutlets with lemon chive butter

This simple recipe for turkey breast cutlets achieves a surprising delicacy.

— 4 servings —

Preheat the grill.

Meanwhile, prepare the turkey cutlets and seasoned butter. Place the turkey breast cutlets on a plate or platter and drizzle them with the olive oil, turning the cutlets in the oil to coat them thoroughly. Set aside. For the seasoned butter, put the butter, lemon zest, lemon juice, and chives in a small bowl. Using a fork, mash together the ingredients. Set aside.

Carefully oil the grill rack. Season the turkey breast slices with salt and black pepper to taste, put them on the grill rack and cook, turning once or twice, until cooked through, 8 to 10 minutes total. Transfer the turkey to serving plates and top it with dollops of the seasoned butter.

4 turkey breast cutlets (1½ pounds total)

2 tablespoons extra-virgin olive oil

4 tablespoons unsalted butter, softened

1 tablespoon grated lemon zest

1 tablespoon lemon juice

1 tablespoon finely chopped fresh chives

Salt

Black pepper

quick tips & variations

* Fresh chervil makes another nice, delicate herbal addition or substitution.
* The butter also goes well with chicken and is surprisingly good on steak.

turkey breast cutlets

Gaining in popularity and availability, turkey breast cutlets—cut from boneless, skinless turkey breast—are sold ready-sliced and prepackaged in most supermarket meat cases today. If you can't find them, ask your butcher to cut them for you. Or buy a boneless, skinless turkey breast and, with a sharp knife, cut it crosswise into slices about ½ inch thick.

smokey barbecued turkey breast cutlets

Our favorite Missouri-style barbecue joint does terrific turkey breast slowly cooked over smoldering hickory logs, resulting in a taste that I've aimed to capture with an astonishingly quick marinade and sauce.

— 4 servings —

4 turkey breast cutlets
   (1½ pounds total)

1 cup tomato ketchup

¼ cup honey, maple syrup, or
   dark corn syrup

1 tablespoon concentrated
   hickory seasoning (Liquid
   Smoke)

   Salt

   Black pepper

Preheat the grill.

Meanwhile, place the turkey breast cutlets on a plate or platter. In a mixing bowl, stir together the ketchup, honey or syrup, and hickory seasoning. Spoon about a third of this sauce over the turkey cutlets and turn them in it to coat them evenly. Divide the remaining sauce into two separate bowls.

Carefully oil the grill rack. Season the turkey breast slices to taste with salt and black pepper. Place the slices on the grill rack and cook, turning once or twice and basting them with another third of the sauce, until cooked through, 8 to 10 minutes total. Transfer the turkey to serving plates and pass the remaining sauce for guests to use as a condiment.

quick tips & variations

* Liquid Smoke is the most popular brand name for a concentrated liquid seasoning extracted from hickory. You'll find it in the seasonings section of many markets. Also look for a similar mesquite smoke seasoning, which may be substituted.
* The same sauce works well for pork.
* The turkey cutlets make excellent sandwiches when served on hamburger rolls that have been brushed with oil or melted butter and toasted on the grill. For a down-home favorite, pile your favorite cole slaw on top of the turkey and inside the bun.

curry and honey turkey breast cutlets with chutney raita

A paste of mild curry powder and mellow honey, along with a quickly composed yogurt sauce, perfectly complements the flavor of turkey breast cutlets.

— 4 servings —

Preheat the grill.

Meanwhile, place the turkey breast cutlets on a plate or platter. In a small bowl, stir together the curry powder, honey, oil, and salt to form a thick, smooth paste. Evenly smear a generous pinch of the paste on both sides of each turkey breast slice, placing the coated slices on a clean plate or platter.

To make the raita, first cut up any large chunks of mango in the chutney into smaller pieces no more than about ¼ inch across. Stir together the chutney, yogurt, and lemon juice. Set aside.

Carefully oil the grill rack. Place the turkey breast slices on the grill rack and cook, turning once or twice, until cooked through, 8 to 10 minutes. Transfer the turkey to serving plates and pass the raita for guests to use as a condiment to taste.

4   turkey breast cutlets
    (1½ pounds total)

1½ tablespoons mild curry powder

1   tablespoon honey

1   tablespoon vegetable oil

½   teaspoon salt

¼   cup Major Grey's mango
    chutney

½   cup plain yogurt

1   tablespoon lemon juice

quick tips & variations

* Seek out a good-quality, imported curry powder. Buy it in small quantities, preferably from an ethnic market with a good turnover of product.
* The same seasoning paste and sauce work well for lamb, pork, or veal.
* The scent of curry powder is hard to wash away. When smearing on the paste you might wish to wear disposable gloves—or use a knife or the back of a spoon.
* Major Grey's is not a brand name for chutney. Rather, it describes a traditional type of sweet, mildly spiced mango chutney available in many different brands. Feel free to substitute a spicier version, or one made with a different type of fruit.

thanksgiving turkey burgers with sage, onion, and cranberry sauce

At any time of year, these easy burgers deliver the satis-fying flavors of Thanksgiving—on a bun!

— 4 servings —

1½ pounds ground turkey

1 small sweet onion, minced

4 teaspoons chicken bouillon powder

1 teaspoon ground sage

Black pepper

4 soft good-quality sandwich rolls or burger buns, split

2 tablespoons unsalted butter, melted

4 ½-inch-thick slices jellied or whole cranberry sauce, canned

Dijon mustard

Mayonnaise

Preheat the grill.

Meanwhile, prepare the turkey burger mixture. In a mixing bowl, using clean hands, lightly combine the ground turkey, onion, bouillon powder, and sage until well blended. Form the mixture into four equal, circular patties about ¾ inch thick. Set aside on a plate. Wash your hands and then brush the cut sides of the rolls with the melted butter.

Carefully oil the grill rack. Season the turkey burgers generously to taste on both sides with black pepper. Place the burgers on the grill rack and cook, turning once, until they are well browned and cooked through, 12 to 14 minutes total. During the last 2 minutes or so, put the roll halves buttered sides down on the grill to toast until golden.

Place a burger on the bottom half of each roll and top it with a slice of cranberry sauce. Serve with Dijon mustard and mayonnaise for guests to add to taste.

quick tips & variations

* Credit goes to my friend Chuck Stewart for showing me how good ground turkey burgers can taste when you amplify their flavor with powdered poultry bouillon. Note that even the best broth mixes will contain plenty of salt, eliminating any need to salt the burgers before cooking.
* For an extra homey touch, I like to serve these burgers on jumbo-sized, split English muffins.

seafood

Simply announce to your guests that you're forgoing burgers or chicken in favor of seafood, and you've taken a big step toward a reputation as a Quick Grill Artist. Fish and shellfish are still viewed by many people as special-occasion ingredients requiring expert know-how to be cooked properly.

That isn't so. In fact, seafood is easy to cook quickly and artistically on the grill, provided you buy it in the right form.

Among shellfish, shrimp and big sea scallops are the perfect choices for quick grilling. Both are widely available, take almost no time to prepare before grilling, and are ready to serve in just minutes. And both have a subtly sweet flavor and tender texture that benefit from a flash of heat and a lick of smoke. The only challenge lies in not leaving shrimp and scallops on the grill too long: get distracted, and they will both turn from moist and tender to dry and chewy in a matter of a minute or two. Many of the shrimp and scallop recipes that follow also work great as appetizers, grilled alongside a slower-cooking meat main course and yielding six to eight servings.

Fish, too, cooks quickly, especially if you buy it in the form of today's widely available fresh fillets. Types of fish that yield thicker fillets—from salmon to tuna, swordfish to sea bass—come out best on the grill, standing up to the relatively rough treatment without drying out or falling apart. Again, your senses will best tell you when grilled fish is perfectly cooked and ready to serve.

spanish-style garlic shrimp skewers

Years ago, on my first visit to Madrid, I enjoyed *gambas al ajillo,* a skillet of sizzling shrimp swimming in garlic-laced olive oil. This simple recipe captures the same dynamic flavors.

— 4 servings —

1½ pounds jumbo shrimp

8 garlic cloves, peeled

½ cup extra-virgin olive oil

Salt

Black pepper

¼ cup finely chopped fresh parsley

1 lemon, cut into 4 wedges

Preheat the grill. If using wooden or bamboo skewers, put them in a bowl of cold water to soak.

Meanwhile, peel and devein the shrimp (see facing page). Press the garlic cloves through a garlic press and into the mixing bowl. Add the olive oil and mix well to coat the shrimp thoroughly. Set aside. Slide the shrimp onto skewers, passing the skewer securely through the head and tail ends of each shrimp. Reserve the oil and garlic left in the bowl.

Carefully oil the grill rack. Season the shrimp with salt and black pepper to taste. Place the skewers on the grill and immediately spoon over them the remaining garlic and oil. Cook, turning once, until the shrimp are plump, pink, and lightly browned, about 5 minutes total. Transfer the shrimp to serving plates, garnish with parsley, and serve with lemon wedges for guests to squeeze over the shrimp.

quicktips &variations

* The combination of seasonings works well with jumbo sea scallops, too.
* If you like, add squares of red bell pepper to the skewers, alternating them with the shrimp.

refreshing, peeling, and deveining shrimp

* Seafood markets and departments often offer shrimp that were frozen at sea and defrosted before sale. If the aroma or appearance of the shrimp give you the impression that they need a little freshening up, soak the shrimp in a bowl of cold, lightly salted water (about ½ teaspoon for 4 cups of water) for 10 minutes right after you peel and devein them. Drain them well, patting dry with paper towels.

* To peel and devein a shrimp, split the shell apart between the rows of legs, then pull the shell and the tail fins away. The vein, actually a gray-to-black digestive tract running along the outer curve, may be removed be slitting the shrimp with a small, sharp knife, then teasing out the vein with your fingertips or the knife tip.

* Alternatively, look in kitchen gadget stores for a plastic shrimp peeling/deveining tool, which resembles the long, curved beak of a kiwi bird. Insert the tool's tip at the head end of a shrimp, where the vein is visible at the outer curve. Then push it in all along the shrimp just inside the shell. In one motion of your wrist, the tool will pry off the shell and strip away the vein, though you may have to pick out small remnants from the shrimp.

* You'll have to pay a little more, but you can often get shrimp already peeled and deveined in quality food stores and seafood shops.

tangy bacon-wrapped apricot shrimp skewers

Just a few simple ingredients add up here to an explosion of flavor. You'll need long skewers for this recipe, to fit six shrimp on each one. Serve with rice pilaf, if you like. You can also offer these as an appetizer, planning on three or four shrimp per person.

— 4 servings —

1½ **pounds jumbo shrimp**

4 **tablespoons smooth apricot jam**

2 **teaspoons lemon juice**

24 **slices smoky bacon**

quicktips
&variations

* Try other tart, tangy preserves such as lemon curd in place of the apricot jam. For a more fiery effect, add a few drops of hot pepper sauce to the jam, or use pepper jelly instead.
* Wrap the shrimp in thinly sliced prosciutto or ham instead of the bacon.

Preheat the grill. If using wooden or bamboo skewers, put them in a bowl of cold water to soak.

Meanwhile, peel and devein the shrimp (see page 109). In a bowl large enough to hold all the shrimp, stir together the apricot jam and lemon juice. Add the shrimp, stirring and tossing to coat them thoroughly.

In a large nonstick skillet, arrange the bacon strips in a single layer. Work in batches if necessary. Place the skillet over medium heat and cook, without turning, until the edges of the bacon just begin to curl, 2 to 3 minutes. Transfer the bacon to paper towels to drain and cool briefly.

Place a shrimp at the narrower end of each bacon slice and roll it up in the bacon. Slide the shrimp onto a skewer, passing the skewer securely through the ends of the bacon on each side of the shrimp. Continue, placing six shrimp on each skewer without letting the shrimp touch each other.

Carefully oil the grill rack. Place the skewers on the grill and cook, turning once, until the bacon is crisply browned and the shrimp are plump and pink, 8 to 10 minutes total.

four-flavor popcorn shrimp

A sweet-savory seasoning mixture gives these plump shrimp a golden-brown, caramelized finish.

— 4 servings —

Preheat the grill. If using wooden or bamboo skewers, put them in a bowl of cold water to soak.

Meanwhile, peel and devein the shrimp (see page 109). If they seem at all in need of freshening, soak them in a bowl of cold, lightly salted water for 10 minutes. Drain them well, patting dry with paper towels.

In a small bowl, stir together the sugar, lemon zest, chili powder, and salt. In another small bowl, stir together the butter and olive oil. Turn a shrimp in the butter-oil mixture to coat it, then turn and press it into the seasoning mixture to coat it well. Gently slide the shrimp onto a skewer, passing the skewer through the head and tail ends to secure the shrimp. Continue with the remaining shrimp.

Carefully oil the grill rack. Place the skewers on the grid and cook, turning once, until the shrimp are cooked through and golden brown, about 5 minutes total. Serve with lemon wedges.

1½ pounds jumbo shrimp

2 tablespoons sugar

1 tablespoon grated lemon zest

2 teaspoons mild pure chili powder or sweet paprika

1 teaspoon salt

2 tablespoons unsalted butter, melted

2 tablespoons extra-virgin olive oil

1 lemon, cut into 4 wedges

quick tips & variations

* For more fiery results, substitute medium-hot to hot chili powder or hot paprika.

soy-and honey-glazed scallop skewers

The combination of Asian flavors adds depth and a hint of complementary sweetness to tender sea scallops.

— 4 servings —

1½ pounds jumbo sea scallops

1 tablespoon soy sauce

1 tablespoon honey

1 tablespoon dry sherry

1 tablespoon Asian toasted sesame oil

1 tablespoon grated fresh ginger root

1 scallion, thinly sliced, for garnish

1 lemon, cut into 4 wedges

Preheat the grill. If using wooden or bamboo skewers, put them in a bowl of cold water to soak.

Trim and discard any tough, white connective tissue from the sides of the scallops. In a mixing bowl, stir together the soy sauce, honey, sherry, sesame oil, and ginger. Add the scallops and turn once to coat them well. Leave them at room temperature. Shortly before cooking, slide the scallops onto skewers, passing the skewer horizontally through the sides of each scallop.

Carefully oil the grill rack. Place the skewers on the grill and cook, turning once, until the scallops are firm and plump, about 5 minutes total. Transfer the skewers to individual serving plates, garnish with the scallions, and serve with lemon wedges for guests to squeeze over their scallops.

quicktips &variations

* The marinade is also delicious with the scallops wrapped in prosciutto, as in the recipe that follows.

* Try the marinade with shrimp, too, or combine jumbo shrimp and sea scallops, alternating them on the skewers.

"fresh" scallops

Be aware that scallops for sale in many markets have been flash-frozen at sea and then defrosted for sale. This can sometimes make them a little bit mushy, which increases their tendency to fall off skewers during grilling. If your scallops seem anything less than firm, consider cooking them on a smaller-mesh grid placed atop your grill rack.

prosciutto-wrapped lemon-basil scallops

Pretty as can be, this dish uses strips of salty-sweet prosciutto to highlight the plump shape, ivory color, and sweet taste of jumbo sea scallops.

— 4 servings —

Preheat the grill. If using wooden or bamboo skewers, put them in a bowl of cold water to soak.

Meanwhile, prepare the scallops. Trim and discard any tough, white connective tissue from the sides of the scallops. In a mixing bowl, stir together the olive oil and lemon juice. Add the scallops and turn once to coat them well. Sprinkle with the black pepper, turning the scallops to coat them evenly.

Shortly before cooking, tear each basil leaf lengthwise in half, one at a time, and place one of the halves around the circular rim of each scallop. Then wrap a strip of prosciutto completely around the rim of the scallop. Slide the wrapped scallop onto a skewer, passing the skewer horizontally through the overlapping ends of the prosciutto slice on one side of the scallop's rim and then out through the rim on the opposite side. Continue with the remaining scallops.

Carefully oil the grill rack. Place the skewers on the grill and cook, turning once, until the scallops are firm and plump, about 5 minutes total.

$1\frac{1}{2}$ **pounds jumbo sea scallops**

2   **tablespoons extra-virgin olive oil**

$1\frac{1}{2}$ **tablespoons lemon juice**

1   **teaspoon black pepper**

8   **thin slices prosciutto, each cut lengthwise into 3 or 4 strips**

12   **fresh basil leaves**

1   **lemon, cut into 4 wedges**

quick tips & variations

* This marinade is also excellent without the basil or prosciutto, and works well with shrimp, too.

dijon-dill salmon

Our dear friend Mary Kay Myers first served us an oven-baked version of this dish, its flavors reminiscent of classic Swedish gravlax, when we were visiting her and her husband Harry at their home near Denver. We made it a standard in our own home, dubbing it "Salmon à la Mary Kay." She smeared the mustard-dill mixture over the fish and baked it in the oven.

——— 4 servings ———

1½ pounds salmon fillet, with skin left on

½ cup Dijon mustard

¼ cup extra-virgin olive oil

¼ cup sugar

6 tablespoons finely chopped fresh dill, or 3 tablespoons dried dill

2 teaspoons white pepper

1 teaspoon salt

1 lemon

Preheat the grill.

Meanwhile, prepare the salmon. With your fingertips, feel along the length of the fillet for the tips of any remaining pin bones. Pull them out, grasping them between your fingertips or using tweezers if necessary.

In a small bowl, stir together the mustard, olive oil, sugar, dill, white pepper, and salt. With the fine holes of a grater/shredder, grate the zest from the lemon into the bowl, taking care to remove only the thin, bright-yellow outermost layer of peel. Cut the lemon in half and squeeze the juice from one half through your outstretched fingers (to catch any seeds) into the bowl. Stir the zest and juice into the mustard mixture. Cut the unsqueezed lemon half into four wedges and set aside.

Place the salmon fillet skin side down on a platter. Evenly smear ½ cup of the Dijon-dill mixture over the top of the fillet. Reserve the remaining mixture.

Carefully oil the grill rack and place the salmon fillet skin side up on the grill. Cover the grill and cook for 5 minutes. Carefully slide two large metal spatulas under the fillet from either end, keeping their leading edges against the grill rack. Flip the fillet over and spoon another ¼ cup of the Dijon-dill mixture over the fish. Cover the fish and grill just until it is cooked through, about 5 minutes more. The salmon should look opaque throughout when the tip of a small, sharp knife blade is inserted between its flakes. If the fish still looks slightly raw, flip it over again and cook 1 to 2 minutes more. With both spatulas, lift and transfer the fillet to a clean serving platter. The salmon's skin may stick to the grill.

Cut the salmon fillet crosswise into individual portions. Serve with lemon wedges and pass the remaining Dijon-dill mixture for guests to use as a sauce, if desired.

quicktips
&variations

* A large, whole, piece of grilled salmon makes a striking presentation at the table. But if you feel anything less than adept at flipping a big piece of salmon fillet, ask the fishmonger instead for individual serving-size pieces, which you'll find easier to flip. Or consider using a hinged grill basket especially made for large fish fillets.
* The Dijon-dill sauce also works well with salmon steaks and with other meaty or flavorful fish fillets, such as swordfish or tuna.

salmon with orange-soy glaze and black pepper

The sweet, salty, and pungent flavors of this recipe's various seasonings add up to a complex, pleasing complement to rich salmon, while giving the deep-pink fish an attractive glaze.

— 4 servings —

1½ pounds salmon fillet, skinned

2 tablespoons orange juice

1 tablespoon honey

2 tablespoons unsalted butter, melted

1 tablespoon grated orange zest

1 tablespoon soy sauce

2 teaspoons ground black pepper

4 orange wedges

quick tips & variations

* A medium-sized orange should provide you with the right amount of juice and zest called for in this recipe.
* For a more casual approach, serve individual portions on slices of sourdough bread that you've drizzled or brushed with olive oil and toasted on the grill. Spicy radish sprouts make a colorful and flavorful garnish for the sandwiches.
* For easier turning of the fish, ask the fishmonger to cut it into individual portions. Or use a hinged grill basket.

Preheat the grill.

Meanwhile, prepare the salmon. With your fingertips, feel along the length of the fillet for the tips of any remaining pin bones. Pull them up, grasping them between your fingertips or using tweezers if necessary.

In a small bowl, stir together the orange juice, honey, butter, orange zest, and soy sauce. Pour half of the mixture into a shallow dish large enough to hold the salmon fillet. Reserve the remainder in the bowl for basting. Turn the fillet in the mixture and leave it, skinned side up, at room temperature.

Carefully oil the grill rack. Generously season the salmon on both sides with black pepper. Place the salmon fillet skinned side up on the grill rack and cook for about 5 minutes. Discard any sauce from the dish in which the salmon marinated. Using a pair of large spatulas, carefully turn the salmon over. Cook it, basting frequently with the reserved sauce, until the salmon looks just opaque at the center when its flakes are separated with the tip of a small, sharp knife, 4 to 5 minutes more.

Transfer to a serving platter, cut into portions, and serve with orange wedges for guests to squeeze over the salmon.

honey-glazed "smoked" salmon

This recipe is amazingly brief. Yet the results taste wonderfully complex, replicating the flavor of good smoked salmon in a fresh salmon fillet that gains a mellow, caramel-colored glaze from honey.

— 4 servings —

4 salmon fillets, skinned (1½ pounds total)

½ cup honey

2 teaspoons concentrated hickory seasoning (Liquid Smoke)

Salt

Black pepper

1½ tablespoons finely chopped fresh chives

1 lemon, cut into wedges

Preheat the grill.

Meanwhile, prepare the salmon and the glaze. With your fingertips, feel along the length of the fillets for the tips of any remaining pin bones. Pull them out, grasping them between your fingertips or using tweezers if necessary. In a small bowl, stir together the honey and hickory seasoning. Set aside.

Carefully oil the grill rack. Season the salmon fillets generously with salt and black pepper to taste. Place the salmon fillets skin side down on the grill. Spoon about one third of the glaze evenly over the salmon. Cover the grill and cook about 3 minutes. Turn the salmon over, spoon on half of the remaining glaze, and grill about 3 minutes more. Turn the salmon a third time and spoon on the rest of the glaze. Grill until the fish is barely cooked through, about 3 minutes more. The salmon should look almost completely opaque when the tip of a small, sharp knife blade is inserted between its flakes, with just a bit of deeper pink remaining at the center. Turn the fish over one final time and grill until the fish is completely done, 1 to 2 minutes more. Lift and transfer the fillets to a clean serving platter or individual serving plates, carefully flipping them skinned side down. Sprinkle the salmon with the chives and distribute the lemon wedges.

quick tips & variations

* Ask the fish dealer to skin the fillets for you.
* You'll find bottles of concentrated hickory seasoning in the seasonings aisle of most markets. Also keep an eye out for mesquite seasoning, which may be substituted.
* The glaze also works well with salmon steaks and with other meaty or flavorful fish fillets, such as swordfish, tuna, or mackerel.
* For a more casual presentation, serve the salmon in hamburger buns or sandwich rolls, split, brushed with olive oil or butter, and briefly toasted on the grill. Serve Dijon mustard, a blend of Dijon mustard and mayonnaise, or a dollop of your favorite tartar sauce as a condiment.

seafood

salmon burgers teriyaki with japanese cucumbers and wasabi-dijon mustard

In many ways these resemble traditional burgers: a juicy patty, a cucumber garnish, a light smear of mustard. But the combination abounds in appealingly light yet highly aromatic Asian flavors.

— 4 servings

japanese cucumbers

- ½ seedless English cucumber (about ½ pound)
- 2 tablespoons rice vinegar
- ½ teaspoon sugar
- ¼ teaspoon salt
- ⅛ teaspoon white pepper

salmon burgers

- 1 garlic clove, peeled
- 1 teaspoon grated fresh ginger
- 1 tablespoon good-quality soy sauce
- 1 tablespoon aji-mirin (a Japanese rice cooking wine)
- 1 teaspoon light brown sugar
- ¼ teaspoon hot chili sesame oil
- 1½ pounds fresh skinless salmon fillet, cut into 1-inch cubes

Preheat the grill.

Meanwhile, make the cucumber salad. With a sharp knife, or using a mandoline if you have one, cut the cucumber crosswise into the thinnest slices you can. Put the slices in a mixing bowl and add the rice vinegar, sugar, salt, and white pepper. Toss them together and set aside.

To prepare the salmon burgers, press the garlic clove through a garlic press and into a food processor fitted with the metal blade. Add the grated ginger, soy sauce, aji-mirin, brown sugar, and hot sesame oil, then pulse the machine briefly to combine. Add the salmon cubes and, if you wish, the cilantro. Pulse the machine on and off several times until the salmon is uniformly but coarsely chopped, resembling coarsely ground beef. With clean hands, form the mixture into four equal, circular patties about 1 inch thick. Place the burgers side by side on a lightly oiled plate or platter.

In a small bowl, stir together the mustard, mayonnaise, and wasabi paste. Set aside. Brush the cut side of each sandwich roll half with the melted butter.

Carefully oil the grill rack. Place the salmon burgers on the grill rack and cook, turning once, until they are golden brown and just cooked through, 7 to 8 minutes total. During the last 2 minutes or so, put the roll halves buttered sides down on the grill to toast until golden.

Place a salmon burger on the bottom half of each roll. Top it with some of the sliced cucumbers. Spread the top halves of the rolls with the mustard-mayonnaise-wasabi mixture to taste.

quick tips
  & variations

* The salmon burgers may seem somewhat soft while you prepare them, but they'll firm up quickly on the grill. Make sure you oil the rack well and evenly. Leave the burgers undisturbed until it is time to turn them, and use a sturdy, wide, thin-bladed metal spatula, keeping its leading edge firmly against the grill rack to help prevent the burgers from sticking. If your grill rack has widely spaced or very thin bars, consider using a smaller mesh grid placed atop the grill rack.
* If time allows, firm up the salmon cubes in the freezer for about half an hour before making the burger mixture. This will promote more even chopping and yield a mixture that is somewhat firmer and easier to shape.
* English, or hothouse, cucumbers are the long, slender, dark-green variety now available in many markets, usually sold shrink-wrapped in plastic. They have mild-tasting skins that don't require peeling, and small, tender seeds that don't have to be scooped out.
* In some Asian markets, you can find ready-to-use wasabi paste in tubes. More traditionally, it is sold as a powder to be mixed with a little water as needed to form a fairly firm paste. Some supermarkets today also include sushi departments that sell small containers of prepared wasabi paste.
* The recipe also works very well with fresh tuna or yellowtail.

2   tablespoons fresh cilantro leaves (optional)

1   tablespoon Dijon mustard

1   tablespoon mayonnaise

¼   teaspoon prepared wasabi paste (Japanese-style horseradish)

4   soft good-quality sandwich rolls or burger buns, split

2   tablespoons unsalted butter, melted

tuna provençale

4 ahi tuna fillets (about 1½ pounds total)

1 (2-ounce) tin anchovy fillets in olive oil, drained

½ cup niçoise olives, pitted

3 tablespoons small capers, rinsed and drained

2 tablespoons finely shredded fresh basil leaves

2 tablespoons extra-virgin olive oil

1½ tablespoons lemon juice

Salt

Black pepper

4 lemon wedges

4 small fresh basil sprigs (optional)

Signature ingredients of the south of France—anchovies, capers, black olives, basil, and olive oil—form a robust, chunky bed of salsa for medium-rare grilled tuna.

— 4 servings —

Preheat the grill. Trim any connective tissue from the sides of the tuna fillets and set them aside at room temperature.

Meanwhile, coarsely chop the anchovies and olives and put them in a mixing bowl. Add the capers, basil, olive oil, and lemon juice, then stir well. Set aside.

Carefully oil the grill rack. Season the tuna fillets generously with salt and black pepper to taste. Place them on the grill and cook, turning them once halfway through, until the fish is done to your liking, 10 to 12 minutes total cooking time for medium.

Spoon the anchovy-olive mixture to form beds on individual serving plates. Place each tuna fillet on top. Garnish with lemon wedges and, if you like, sprigs of fresh basil.

quick tips & variations

* The anchovy-olive mixture goes very well with other meaty or robust fish, such as swordfish or salmon.
* You'll find jars of small, black, brine-cured niçoise-style olives among the pickles in well-stocked supermarkets, and you'll find them sold loose in upscale deli cases. An olive pitter, a handheld device that grips the olive and pushes out its pit with one squeeze, can make quick work of pitting the olives. Alternatively, just cut off the olives' flesh from the pit with a small, sharp knife. In a pinch, widely available jars of already pitted Kalamata olives may be substituted.
* If you like, add a clove or two of minced garlic to the anchovy-olive mixture.

seared ahi
with citrus soy dip

A sushi bar favorite is transformed into a stunning light main course or appetizer for a grilled meal.

— 4 to 6 servings —

Preheat the grill.

Meanwhile, prepare the tuna and dipping sauce. If the ahi fillets are large, cut them lengthwise into blocks about 2 inches thick. Put them in a bowl. In another bowl, stir together the soy sauce, orange juice, lemon juice, rice vinegar, and sugar until the sugar dissolves. Pour about a third of this mixture over the tuna and turn the tuna in it to coat it. Set the tuna and the remaining sauce aside. Prepare beds of radish sprouts on individual serving plates. Mound a little pile of pickled ginger on one side of each plate and a little mound of wasabi paste on the other side. Set out a small sauce dish at each serving place for the dipping sauce.

Carefully oil the grill rack. Remove the ahi from its marinade, shake off any excess marinade, and discard the marinade in which the tuna sat. Lightly brush the tuna with the sesame oil. Grill the tuna, turning occasionally, until evenly browned on all sides but still rare to medium rare in the center, 1 to 2 minutes per side.

Remove the grilled ahi to a cutting board. With a sharp knife, cut it crosswise into slices about 1/3 inch thick. Arrange the slices to overlap on the beds of radish sprouts, then sprinkle them with sesame seeds. Pass the reserved sauce for guests to spoon into their individual sauce dishes, to be seasoned with dabs of wasabi paste to taste and used as a dip for the tuna slices, each bite accompanied by the garnishes of pickled ginger and radish sprouts on each plate.

1½ pounds sushi-grade ahi tuna

½ cup soy sauce

½ cup orange juice

¼ cup lemon juice

¼ cup rice vinegar

2 teaspoons sugar

2½ to 3 ounces radish sprouts

¼ cup pink pickled ginger

2 teaspoons wasabi paste

1 tablespoon Asian toasted sesame oil

1 tablespoon toasted or black sesame seeds

quick tips & variations

* Make this dish only when the freshest, sushi-grade ahi tuna is available.
* Many supermarkets today have freshly made sushi counters that sell small containers of pink pickled ginger and already prepared wasabi paste. You can also find both in the Asian foods section of the market. The ginger is sold in jars, and the wasabi either in tubes or as a powder that must be mixed with cold water, following package instructions, to form the paste.
* If you like, transform this dish into a salad by arranging a bed of mixed baby greens beneath the radish sprouts and spooning the sauce over the tuna and greens.
* A few slices of ripe Hass avocado make a luscious addition to each serving.

swordfish veracruzano and tomato-olive-pepper salsa

Fish prepared in the style of Veracruz, Mexico, usually comes with a cooked sauce of tomatoes, green olives, and peppers. The swiftly made salsa that accompanies this grilled fish captures the same combination of flavors.

— 4 servings —

tomato-olive-pepper salsa

- 2 large, firm, ripe Roma tomatoes, cored, halved, seeded, and cut into ¼-inch dice (about 1¼ cups)
- ½ red onion, cut into ¼-inch dice
- ½ to 1 jalapeño chili, stemmed, seeded, and minced
- ½ cup thinly sliced pitted green olives
- ½ cup diced roasted red bell pepper
- ¼ cup finely chopped fresh cilantro
- 2 tablespoons lime juice
- 1 tablespoon extra-virgin olive oil
- ¼ teaspoon salt

swordfish

- 4 1-inch-thick swordfish fillets (1½ pounds total)
- 1 tablespoon extra-virgin olive oil
- 1 teaspoon mild to medium-hot pure chili powder
- ½ teaspoon ground cumin

  Salt

  Black pepper

- 1 lime, cut into 4 wedges

Preheat the grill.

Meanwhile, make the salsa and prepare the swordfish. For the salsa, in a mixing bowl stir together the tomatoes, red onion, jalapeño to taste, olives, bell pepper, cilantro, lime juice, olive oil, and salt. Cover with plastic wrap and refrigerate.

To prepare the swordfish, first use a sharp knife to cut any skin from one side of the fillets. Put the fish in a shallow dish and rub it on both sides with the olive oil. Sprinkle the chili powder and cumin evenly over both sides. Set aside at room temperature.

When the grill is ready, season the swordfish with salt and black pepper to taste. Carefully oil the grill rack. Place the swordfish on the grill. Cook until done to your liking, 12 to 14 minutes. Transfer the swordfish to individual serving plates and heap the salsa over the fish, or alongside it. Serve with lime wedges.

quick tips & variations

* The seasonings and salsa go very well with other meaty, flavorful fish, such as sea bass, halibut, or snapper.
* Feel free to use stuffed, pitted green olives of your choice. Especially good are those stuffed with pimentos, onions, anchovies, or even jalapeño chilies.
* For an especially attractive presentation, spread the salsa on individual serving plates and place the grilled swordfish on top.

seafood

moroccan swordfish kebabs

This unusual combination of sweet and spicy seasonings is especially well suited to the meaty flavor of swordfish fillets.

———— 4 servings ———

Preheat the grill. If using wooden or bamboo skewers, put them in a bowl of cold water to soak.

Meanwhile, prepare the swordfish. Put the swordfish cubes into a mixing bowl, add the olive oil and lemon juice, then toss gently to coat them well. In a separate bowl, stir together the salt, cumin, paprika, ginger, black pepper, and cinnamon. Set aside. Shortly before grilling, slide the swordfish cubes onto skewers, alternating them with red and green bell pepper squares and spacing the pieces slightly apart. Sprinkle the kebabs evenly with the spice mixture.

Carefully oil the grill rack. Place the kebabs on the grill and cook, turning them every 2 minutes or so, until the swordfish is opaque throughout when a cube is pierced with the tip of a small, sharp knife, 10 to 12 minutes total. Serve with lemon wedges.

1½ pounds swordfish fillets, cut into 1½-inch cubes

2 tablespoons extra-virgin olive oil

1 tablespoon lemon juice

½ teaspoon salt

½ teaspoon ground cumin

½ teaspoon sweet paprika

½ teaspoon ground ginger

½ teaspoon black pepper

¼ teaspoon ground cinnamon

1 red bell pepper, stemmed, seeded, and cut into 1-inch squares

1 green bell pepper, stemmed, seeded, and cut into 1-inch squares

2 lemons, cut into wedges

quick tips & variations

* The kebabs work very well with other firm, meaty fish, such as sea bass or tuna.
* To give the recipe an unexpected but pleasing tropical twist, add 1-inch chunks of fresh pineapple to the skewers.

swordfish with anchovy-lemon butter

Just a dab of anchovy paste, or the equivalent amount of finely minced canned anchovy fillets, adds alluring aromatic flavor to a seasoned butter for meaty swordfish.

— 4 servings —

4 swordfish fillets (about 1½ pounds total)

4 tablespoons unsalted butter, softened

2 tablespoons lemon juice

1 tablespoon anchovy paste

Salt

Black pepper

4 lemon wedges

Preheat the grill. With a small, sharp knife, cut off any skin that might have been left along one side of each swordfish fillet.

Meanwhile, in a small bowl, use a fork to mash together the butter, lemon juice, and anchovy paste until smooth. Set aside.

Carefully oil the grill rack. Season the swordfish fillets generously with salt and black pepper to taste. Place them on the grill and cook, turning them once halfway through, until the fish is cooked through and flaky, 10 to 12 minutes total.

Transfer the swordfish fillets to individual serving plates and top each one with a dollop of the anchovy butter. Garnish with lemon wedges.

quicktips &variations

* The anchovy butter is excellent served atop other robust fish, such as tuna or salmon, and is also surprisingly good with grilled veal.
* If you like, add a little finely chopped fresh parsley or shredded basil to the butter, or scatter either or both of these herbs over the cooked fillets after you've topped them with the butter.

sea bass and mushroom kebabs with ginger and scallions

Bright, eye-opening Asian flavors enliven these simple kebabs made from firm, white-fleshed fish fillets.

———— 4 servings ————

Preheat the grill. If using wooden or bamboo skewers, put them in a bowl of cold water to soak.

Meanwhile, prepare the kebabs. Put the chunks of sea bass in a mixing bowl with the mushrooms. Put the white parts of the scallions, the ginger, and the oil in a food processor fitted with the metal blade and pulse the machine several times, just until the vegetables are finely chopped but not yet a paste. Scrape the mixture over the fish and mushrooms and stir well to coat them. Set aside. Just before cooking, thread the fish and mushrooms in alternating pieces onto skewers and season with salt and pepper to taste.

Carefully oil the grill rack. Put the kebabs on the grill and cook, turning several times, until the fish and mushrooms are golden and the fish flakes when tested with the tip of a knife, about 10 minutes. Garnish with the green parts of the scallions and serve with lemon wedges.

1½ pounds sea bass fillets, cut into 1-inch chunks

¾ pound medium-sized cultivated mushrooms, stems trimmed

8 scallions, white parts cut into 1-inch chunks, green parts cut into thin slices

2 tablespoons coarsely chopped fresh ginger

¼ cup canola oil or vegetable oil

Salt

Black pepper

1 lemon, cut into wedges

quick tips & variations

* Substitute other firm, white-fleshed fish, such as swordfish, halibut, or escolar.
* Try the seasoning mixture with jumbo shrimp or sea scallops.

blackened red snapper with quick tropical salsa

A Cajun-inspired seasoning blend adds a blast of flavor to fish fillets, while a refreshing salsa tempers the heat.

4 servings

quick tropical salsa

1 ripe, fresh mango, peeled, pitted, and coarsely chopped

½ to 1 small red or green fresh serrano chili

¼ red onion, minced

4 tablespoons coarsely chopped fresh cilantro

Juice of ½ lime

Salt

blackened red snapper

4 skinned red snapper fillets (1½ pounds)

2 tablespoons extra-virgin olive oil

2 teaspoons sweet paprika

1 teaspoon dried oregano

½ teaspoon cayenne pepper

½ teaspoon ground cumin

½ teaspoon onion salt

½ teaspoon garlic salt

½ teaspoon black pepper

½ teaspoon sugar

Lemon or lime wedges

Preheat the grill.

Meanwhile, prepare the salsa, stirring together the mango, chili pepper to taste, red onion, cilantro, and lime juice. Season to taste with a little salt. Cover and refrigerate until serving time.

To prepare the fish, place the fillets on a large, flat plate or platter. Drizzle them with the olive oil and turn to coat them evenly. In a small bowl, prepare the blackening spices, stirring together the paprika, oregano, cayenne, cumin, onion and garlic salts, black pepper, and sugar. Sprinkle the spices evenly over both sides of the fish fillets.

Carefully oil the grill rack. Place the fish fillets on the grill and cook, turning them once halfway through, until their coating is blackened and the fish flakes when tested with the tip of a small, sharp knife, 13 to 15 minutes total cooking time.

Transfer the fish fillets to individual serving plates, garnish with lemon or lime wedges, and pass the Quick Tropical Salsa on the side for guests to add to their plates to taste.

quick tips
& variations

* Other firm, white fish fillets, such as sea bass or halibut, also work well. Or try the recipe with salmon fillets.
* In a pinch, substitute a commercial Cajun spice blend for the seasoning mixture in the recipe.
* To prepare the mango quickly, cut a thick slice from each side of the fruit, right up to the large, oblong, flat pit. With a sharp knife tip, repeatedly score the flesh of each slice in a small grid pattern, cutting down to, but not through, the thick skin. Then press on the skin side to pop out the grid of fruit, slicing the pieces from the skin. Peel the remaining skin from around the edge of the pit, cut off the flesh, and chop it into smaller pieces if necessary.
* The fish and salsa are also terrific served in tortillas warmed on the grill. For soft tacos, fold corn tortillas around the filling; for burritos, wrap the fish and salsa inside large flour tortillas.

lemon-and-dill-scented trout in grape leaves

Whole boned trout wrapped and grilled in grape leaves makes a beautiful presentation. You can find grape leaves in jars in the pickle aisle or the imported foods section of well-stocked markets. The leaves keep the fish moist and impart their own delicate flavor; they come out lightly charred, and can be nibbled along with the fish.

— 4 servings —

4   whole boneless trout, with or without their heads

36 to 48 bottled grape leaves, drained and patted dry with paper towels

½   cup extra-virgin olive oil

Salt

Black pepper

2   lemons, 1 very thinly sliced, seeds removed, and 1 cut into wedges

8   large sprigs fresh dill

quicktips &variations

* Though it looks like it may be a small amount, an 8-ounce jar of grape leaves will contain more than four dozen individual leaves, tightly stacked and rolled together—more than enough for this recipe.
* Ask your fish dealer to bone the trout for you.
* Fillets of fish cut into slender pieces resembling the shape of trout, including sea bass, halibut, and salmon, may be prepared in the same way, with the lemon slices and dill placed directly atop the fish and inside the grape leaf package.

Preheat the grill.

Meanwhile, prepare the trout. Rinse the fish inside and out with cold running water and pat them dry. For each trout, arrange a bed of 9 or 12 grape leaves (depending on whether the fish are, respectively, headless or still with heads). Overlap the leaves in three rows, with their wide stems all on the bottom facing upward, to form a rectangle large enough to completely enclose the fish. Lay the fish crosswise along the center of the grape leaves. Open the trout's cavity. Drizzle the inside with 1 tablespoon of olive oil, sprinkle generously with salt and black pepper to taste, and stuff with three lemon slices and two dill sprigs. Close the fish compactly, then fold the bottom and top grape leaves up around the fish to enclose it. Rub the exterior of the package with 1 tablespoon of olive oil to help seal it. Set aside.

Carefully oil the grill rack. Place the trout on the grill perpendicular to the rack's wires. Grill the fish until the grape leaves are evenly browned and the fish of one trout flakes easily when a knife tip is inserted, 14 to 16 minutes total, turning them once carefully with a spatula or tongs midway through. Carefully transfer to individual serving plates and garnish with lemon wedges, letting each guest carefully unwrap the grape leaves and peel back the now-loosened skin to expose the trout meat.

vegetables

In my long grilling experience, I've learned a simple lesson that perhaps more than any other can easily transform anyone into a Quick Grill Artist: Serve a hot-off-the-grill accompaniment alongside your main dish and you'll be thought to have achieved an act of high creativity.

Vegetable side dishes have that power. The recipes for them in this chapter are expressly designed to help you make a big impression with very little effort. Whenever you plan a grilled meal, sort through the following pages after you've selected your main dish, searching for one or more accompaniments whose flavors, textures, and appearance best complement what you'll be serving. Compare the cooking times of the recipes you choose to determine the optimum moment to add the vegetables to the grill so that they'll be ready to serve with the main course. Or, if there isn't enough space on the grill rack, grill the vegetables first and then set them aside; most of them will be just fine served lukewarm.

A number of these vegetable dishes may also play the role of a first course, and I've indicated those that are best suited for this purpose. I'm especially fond of composing an Italian antipasto-style platter of assorted grilled vegetables.

Many of these recipes, of course, can become main courses in their own right if you or one or more of your guests is a vegetarian. Compose a grilled meal of several companionable vegetable dishes, adding grill-toasted bread or some rice from the kitchen to round out your menu.

tricolore tomato stacks

The ingredients of a classic Italian salad—tomatoes, mozzarella, and basil—are recombined here into a colorful, easy side dish for Mediterranean-style meats, poultry, or seafood. You could also add them to a grilled antipasto platter.

———— 4 servings ————

2 firm, ripe beefsteak tomatoes (about 1 pound total weight)

1½ tablespoons extra-virgin olive oil

Salt

Black pepper

½ teaspoon sugar

8 whole fresh basil leaves

½ pound mozzarella cheese, cut into 4 slices

Preheat the grill.

Meanwhile, prepare the tomatoes. Trim the top and bottom from each tomato and then cut each one crosswise in half, yielding a total of four thick slices. Put the slices on a plate, drizzle them with the olive oil, and turn them in the oil to coat them thoroughly.

Carefully oil the grill rack. Sprinkle the tomatoes on both sides with salt and black pepper to taste, and the sugar. Place them on the grill rack and cook until their undersides are golden, 1 to 2 minutes. With a spatula, turn the tomato slices over. Immediately top each slice with 2 basil leaves and a slice of mozzarella. Cover the grill and cook until the cheese has begun to melt, 3 to 4 minutes more. Transfer the tomatoes to a serving plate and serve immediately or at room temperature.

quick tips & variations

* This recipe works best when the tomatoes you use are good and firm so they hold their shape well on the grill. The thicker slices ensure that they won't fall apart.
* The sugar included in the recipe serves to heighten the tomatoes' naturally sweet flavor. But if your tomatoes already taste especially good (take a bite from the trimmed top or bottom to test), you can leave the sugar out.
* In place of the basil leaves, smear each tomato slice with a couple teaspoons of good-quality store-bought pesto sauce.

panzanella
kebabs

A classic Italian salad of tomatoes and bread was the inspiration for this delicious little accompaniment for Italian- or French-style meat, poultry, or seafood dishes.

— 4 servings —

Preheat the grill. If using wooden or bamboo skewers, put them in a bowl of cold water to soak.

Put the bread cubes and cherry tomatoes in a mixing bowl. Drizzle them all over with the olive oil and toss gently but well to coat them all. Sprinkle them evenly with the salt. If you'd like a touch of garlic, toss it in as well.

Thread the bread cubes and tomatoes onto four skewers, starting and ending each with a bread cube to anchor the tomatoes in place.

Carefully oil the grill rack. Place the skewers on the grill and cook, turning several times, until the bread cubes are evenly browned, 4 to 5 minutes total. Transfer the skewers to a platter or individual serving plates. Serve hot or lukewarm.

16 large cubes (about 1½ inches) sourdough or rustic bread

12 firm but ripe cherry tomatoes, stems removed

¼ cup extra-virgin olive oil

¼ teaspoon salt

1 garlic clove, finely minced (optional)

quicktips
&variations

* This recipe works especially well if the bread is a day or two old, slightly stale, and firm. If your bread is fresh, try to use cubes that have some sturdy crust on them, passing the skewers through the crusty side.
* Cutting the bread cubes slightly bigger than the diameter of the tomatoes will ensure that the tomatoes cook without scorching or sticking.
* Substitute golden cherry tomatoes for some or all of the red cherry tomatoes.
* To return the dish back to its salad roots, slide the grilled bread cubes and tomatoes off the skewers into a mixing bowl. Sprinkle with a tablespoon or two of balsamic vinegar or lemon juice, add 1 tablespoon each of chopped fresh basil and Italian parsley, and toss well before serving.

the virtues of ready-to-use vegetables

Busy grill cooks who value time above all else can take advantage today of a growing number of vegetables sold in the supermarket produce section that come cleaned and prepared for instant use in the kitchen.

Little plastic-wrapped baskets of cherry tomatoes, all washed and stemmed, are a given nowadays. Look, too, for such items as uniformly perfect cultivated mushrooms, neatly trimmed and wiped clean; corn on the cob that has been stripped of its husks and silk; big bouquets of broccoli florets free of their tough stalks; and impeccably groomed little potatoes with not a speck of dirt to be seen on their skins.

All these conveniences come at a price, both literally and figuratively. You'll pay more for the extra processing. And an argument could be made that such items may be a tad less fresh and, therefore, less flavorful and nutritious than regular produce. But for most cooks who are busy enough to consider buying ready-to-use vegetables, the benefits far outweigh such minor drawbacks.

parmesan-herb stuffed peppers

Serve these with red meat or poultry, or as part of a grilled antipasto platter.

— 4 servings —

Preheat the grill.

Meanwhile, stand each pepper upright on a cutting board and, with a sharp knife, quarter the pepper vertically. Cut out the stem and remove all the seeds and veins from inside each pepper piece.

In a small mixing bowl, stir together the Parmesan, olive oil, basil, parsley, and chives. Set aside.

Carefully oil the grill rack. Place the pepper pieces skin sides up on the grill rack and cook for about 5 minutes. With tongs or a spatula, flip them over. Immediately spoon the cheese-herb mixture inside each pepper piece and continue cooking until the undersides of the peppers are well browned and the cheese mixture is hot and bubbly. Serve hot or lukewarm.

2 red, yellow, or orange bell peppers

6 tablespoons freshly grated Parmesan cheese

2 tablespoons extra-virgin olive oil

2 tablespoons finely shredded fresh basil leaves

2 tablespoons finely chopped fresh Italian parsley

2 tablespoons finely chopped fresh chives

quick tips & variations

* Any color of bell pepper will work well for this recipe, although you'll get the sweetest flavor from red, yellow, or orange bell peppers.
* When choosing peppers, look for well-formed specimens that have four discernible sides to them. These will more easily give you the four pieces per pepper called for in the recipe.
* Try substituting creamy goat cheese for some or all of the Parmesan.

vegetables

133

miso-ginger eggplant

Miso paste, made from fermented soybeans and widely available in the refrigerated sections of supermarkets and Asian food stores, lends a suave richness to eggplant, which becomes meltingly tender on the grill. This recipe is outstanding with grilled lamb or chicken.

— 4 servings

2 large, slender Asian eggplants (about ¾ pound total weight)

¼ cup yellow or red miso paste

2 tablespoons soy sauce

1 tablespoon Asian toasted sesame oil

½ tablespoon grated fresh ginger root

Preheat the grill.

Meanwhile, prepare the eggplants. Trim off their stems and flower ends and cut them lengthwise into slices about ⅓ inch thick. In a small bowl, stir together the miso paste, soy sauce, sesame oil, and ginger. Smear the mixture all over the eggplant slices. Set aside.

Carefully oil the grill rack. Place the eggplant slices perpendicular to the grill rack's wires and cook them until tender and golden brown, turning them once with a metal spatula, 10 to 12 minutes total cooking time. Serve immediately.

quick tips & variations

* Slender Asian eggplants have fewer seeds, more tender skins, and a milder flavor than the familiar big globe eggplants. But a smaller specimen of this more common variety may be substituted.
* Yellow miso paste has a milder flavor than red miso. Either will work fine for this recipe.
* To prevent sticking when turning the eggplant slices, use a sturdy metal spatula, keeping its edge against the grill rack.

rustic
ratatouille

All the components of ratatouille, the classic French vegetable stew, come together surprisingly quickly on the
grill, which adds an edge of smoky flavor and crisp texture. Serve with grilled meats, poultry, or seafood.

— 4 to 6 servings —

¾ pound slender Asian-style
   eggplant

1 small red (Spanish) onion

2 firm, ripe Roma tomatoes

½ pound zucchini

½ cup extra-virgin olive oil

1½ tablespoons dried oregano

½ tablespoon salt

   Black pepper

4 shallots, minced

2 tablespoons finely shredded
   fresh basil leaves

2 tablespoons finely chopped
   fresh Italian parsley

Preheat the grill.

Meanwhile, prepare the vegetables. Trim the eggplants
and cut them lengthwise into 1-inch-thick slices. Peel and
trim the onion and cut it crosswise into 1-inch-thick slices,
securing its rings by pushing three wooden toothpicks,
evenly spaced, in from the side to the center. Core the
tomatoes and cut them in half lengthwise. Cut each zucchini lengthwise in half. Arrange the vegetables on a large
platter and drizzle them all over with the olive oil, turning
the pieces to coat them evenly. Crumble the oregano
evenly over the vegetables, turning them to season both
sides. Season them on both sides with the salt and black
pepper to taste.

Carefully oil the grill rack. Add the vegetables in a single
layer and cook until they are tender and golden brown,
turning each piece occasionally, basting with the oil
remaining on the platter, and removing each piece back
to the platter as it is done, about 15 minutes total cooking
time. Remove the toothpicks from the onion slices.
Quickly cut all the vegetables into rough bite-sized
chunks, and toss them together on the platter, adding the
shallots, basil, and parsley and adjusting the seasoning
with a little more salt to taste.

quick tips
& variations

* The ratatouille may be served hot, warm,
  or at room temperature. Store leftovers in
  a covered container in the refrigerator;
  they'll be excellent cold the next day.
* Add sweet red bell pepper, or sharper
  green bell pepper, to the mixture if you
  like.
* Substitute a sweet yellow onion, such as a
  Maui, Vidalia, Walla Walla, or Texas 1015s
  for the red onion.
* In place of some or all of the shallots,
  substitute finely minced garlic.

asparagus with orange gremolata

Gremolata is a traditional northern Italian seasoning mixture of chopped fresh garlic, parsley, and grated orange or lemon zest. Sprinkled over food just before serving, it lends a sudden burst of aromatic flavor—perfect for asparagus. The vegetable makes a spectacular spring or summer first course, or a great companion to grilled meat, poultry, or seafood.

— 4 servings —

1 **pound plump white or green asparagus spears**

3 **tablespoons extra-virgin olive oil**

2 **tablespoons orange juice**

2 **garlic cloves, peeled**

2 **tablespoons finely chopped fresh Italian parsley**

1 **tablespoon grated orange zest**

Salt

Black pepper

quicktips
&variations

* Big, sturdy asparagus spears are easy to grill because you can place them at right angles to the wires of the rack without fear of them falling into the fire. If the asparagus are smaller or more slender, place them on a finer-mesh grill rack on top of the grill.

Preheat the grill.

Meanwhile, prepare the asparagus and the gremolata. With a small, sharp knife, trim off the tough ends of the stalks. With a vegetable peeler, pare off any tough outer skin, stopping 2 inches or so below the asparagus tips. Put the asparagus in a microwave-proof dish big enough to hold them horizontally. Add 2 tablespoons water, cover, and microwave just until tender-crisp, about 2 minutes. Drain well, pat the spears dry with paper towels, drizzle evenly with the 3 tablespoons of the olive oil and the orange juice, toss lightly to coat them well, and set aside.

For the gremolata, press the garlic cloves through a garlic press and into a small bowl. Add the parsley and orange zest, and stir to combine. Set aside.

Carefully oil the grill rack. Season the asparagus spears generously with salt and black pepper to taste. Place the spears at right angles to the bars of the grill rack. Cook the asparagus, turning them two or three times, until they are tender and beginning to turn golden brown, 4 to 6 minutes total cooking time. Transfer them to a platter and immediately scatter the gremolata mixture over them before serving.

baby artichokes
with garlic,
olive oil,
and lemon

Inspired by southern French cooking, these skewers of tiny artichokes go very well with grilled meat, poultry, or seafood. They may also be served as part of a grilled antipasto plate.

— 4 servings —

1 lemon, cut into 6 wedges

24 baby artichokes, each 2½ to 3 inches from base to tip

6 tablespoons extra-virgin olive oil

3 garlic cloves, peeled

1 teaspoon sea salt or regular salt

1 teaspoon black pepper

2 tablespoons chopped fresh Italian parsley, basil, or a mix

Preheat the grill. If using wooden or bamboo skewers, put them in a bowl of cold water to soak.

Meanwhile, prepare the artichokes. Fill a large mixing bowl with cold water. Squeeze two lemon wedges into the water. Using a small, sharp knife, pare each artichoke: first, cut off the stem flush with the base; next, starting at the base, pull off the leaves until you get about halfway up the artichoke, exposing paler yellow-green flesh beneath; finally, cut off the top, green half of the artichoke, leaving a whole baby artichoke heart 1 to 1½ inches in diameter. Drop the artichoke heart into the lemon water.

When all the artichokes are ready, drain them well and pat them dry with paper towels. Dry out the bowl, add the olive oil, and press the garlic cloves through a garlic press and into the oil. Stir to mix, adding the artichoke hearts and turning them in the garlic-oil mixture to coat them. Thread the artichoke hearts on skewers, passing the skewer through the center of its top, leafy end and out the center of its base. Reserve the garlicky oil.

Carefully oil the grill rack. Season the artichoke skewers with sea salt and black pepper, place them on the grill, and cook until they are golden brown, turning occasionally and basting them a few times with the reserved olive oil-garlic mixture, 13 to 15 minutes total cooking time. Garnish them with the fresh herbs and serve with lemon wedges for guests to squeeze over them to taste.

quick tips & variations

* Use slender skewers and baby artichokes on the larger side. This way, you'll run a lesser risk of splitting the artichokes during skewering.

sage-dusted
sweet onion
slices

These onions make a simply wonderful accompaniment to grilled pork, turkey, or other meats or poultry.

———— 4 servings ————

2 sweet onions (about 1 pound total weight)

4 tablespoons unsalted butter, melted

1 teaspoon ground sage

1 teaspoon salt

Preheat the grill. Put about two dozen sturdy wooden toothpicks into a bowl of cold water to soak for a few minutes.

Meanwhile, prepare the onion slices. Cut off the root and leaf ends of the onion, then cut the onion into slices about ¾ inch thick. Remove the peel from each slice. Carefully push three wooden toothpicks into each slice from its side toward the center to secure the rings during grilling. Place the slices on a plate and coat them on both sides with the melted butter. With your fingertips, dust the onions with the sage and then sprinkle the salt over both sides of the slices.

Carefully oil the grill rack. Place the onion slices on the grill and cook, turning once, until they are golden brown, 10 to 12 minutes total. Remove from the grill to a serving dish and carefully pull out the toothpicks from each slice before serving.

quicktips
&variations

* Sweet onions such as Mauis, Vidalias, Walla Wallas, or Texas 1015s work best for this recipe, which gains in rich flavor as the onions' natural sugars caramelize on the grill.
* To encourage extra caramelization, sprinkle the onion slices with a pinch of sugar when you season them with the sage and salt.
* The recipe will also work well with Spanish (red) onions or any mild, brown-skinned variety.

balsamic-glazed red onions

The sweet, rich, tangy flavor of balsamic vinegar makes it a natural for basting mild, sweet onions, producing a beautiful accompaniment for grilled meat or seafood.

——— 4 servings ———

2 small- to medium-sized red (Spanish) onions

¼ cup good-quality balsamic vinegar

2 tablespoons extra-virgin olive oil

Salt

Black pepper

Preheat the grill.

Meanwhile, prepare the onions. With a sharp knife, cut each onion in half along its equator. Then, barely trim the rounded ends, so that each half is neat but will hold together. Slit and remove the skin from each half. In a shallow dish large enough to hold the onion halves side by side, stir together the vinegar and oil. Place the onions cut sides down in the mixture. Set aside.

Carefully oil the grill rack. Season the onions to taste with salt and pepper and place them cut sides down along the sides of the grill, away from the hot center of the fire. Cook until their cut sides begin to brown, about 5 minutes. Turn them over and continue to grill, basting every minute or so with a little of the vinegar-oil mixture, until the rounded sides of the onions are well browned and the onions are tender, about 10 minutes more. Spoon on the last of the vinegar and oil and turn the onions over to finish browning their cut sides and set the glaze, 1 to 2 minutes more. Serve hot or at room temperature.

quick tips & variations

* The onions are a natural for grilling alongside steaks or other large cuts of meat.
* The recipe also works well with sweet yellow onions such as Mauis, Vidalias, Walla Wallas, or Texas 1015s.

cantina
scallions

Authentic Mexican *taquerías* sometimes include a few of these easy-to-make, sweet-and-smoky onions alongside tacos or burritos filled with grilled beef, chicken, or seafood. Serve these as a side dish with any grilled main course.

———— 4 servings ————

1   bunch scallions (about 12 scallions, 4 to 6 ounces total)

2   to 3 tablespoons extra-virgin olive oil

Salt

Black pepper

1   lime, cut into wedges

Preheat the grill.

Meanwhile, prepare the scallions. With a small, sharp knife, trim off their roots flush with the white bulb. Trim an inch or two off the green tops and remove any damaged or blemished leaves. Put the scallions in a shallow dish large enough to hold them lengthwise. Drizzle them with just enough of the oil to coat them well, and turn them in the oil until evenly coated. Season generously with salt and black pepper to taste.

Carefully oil the grill rack. Spread the scallions side by side on the grill rack and cook, turning frequently, until they are tender and slightly charred, about 10 minutes. Serve with lime wedges to be squeezed over them.

quick tips
& variations

*   When shopping, look for medium-sized scallions. Very thin ones may go limp before they're well browned, while big scallions could burn before they're cooked through.
*   For an extra touch of heat, add a light dusting of mild or hot pure chili powder along with the salt and pepper.
*   Making Bloody Marys to serve at a back-yard grill party? Use one of these to replace the celery stick that usually juts from the glass. You may want to reduce the grilling time slightly, so the scallions hold their shape better.

vegetables

140

chinese chili-sesame scallions

Serve these rich-flavored, spicy onions with any Asian-inspired main course.

——————————— 4 servings ———

1 bunch scallions (about 12 scallions, 4 to 6 ounces total)

2 to 3 tablespoons hot chili sesame oil

Salt

Black pepper

1 teaspoon toasted sesame seeds or black sesame seeds (optional)

Preheat the grill.

Meanwhile, prepare the scallions. With a small, sharp knife, trim off their roots flush with the white bulb. Trim an inch or two off the green tops and remove any damaged or blemished leaves. Put the scallions in a shallow dish large enough to hold them lengthwise. Drizzle them with just enough of the oil to coat them well, and turn them in the oil until evenly coated. Season generously with salt and black pepper to taste.

Carefully oil the grill rack. Spread the scallions side by side on the grill rack and cook, turning frequently, until they are tender and slightly charred, about 10 minutes. Remove them to a platter and, if you like, sprinkle with sesame seeds before serving.

quicktips & variations

* If you'd prefer the scallions less spicy, substitute plain Asian toasted sesame oil.

migas

Simple in name and in preparation, this traditional Mexican recipe nonetheless produces profoundly delicious corn to serve with grilled meat or poultry.

— 4 servings ⌐

4 ears fresh sweet corn, husks and silks removed

4 teaspoons extra-virgin olive oil

1 tablespoon lime juice

½ teaspoon mild pure chili powder

¼ teaspoon salt

quicktips &variations

* This recipe will be at its best if you use freshly picked corn, preferably bought from a farm stand or farmers' market on the day it was picked. If the corn tastes less than sweet and fresh, try sprinkling in a little sugar along with the other seasonings.
* For contrasting color and flavor, grill some stemmed and seeded red or green bell pepper halves along with the corn, then dice them and add to the mixture.
* Finely chopped fresh cilantro or chives are also good additions.
* For another popular Mexican variation, crumble some fresh Mexican cheese such as cotija over the corn just before serving. Mild feta cheese makes a good substitute.

Preheat the grill.

Meanwhile, put the ears of corn in a microwave-proof dish, add 2 tablespoons of water, cover, and microwave just until the corn is tender, about 4 minutes. Drain well and pat the ears dry with paper towels. Set aside.

Just before grilling, rub the ears of corn all over with the olive oil. Place them on the grill rack and cook, turning frequently, until the corn kernels turn a deep golden brown color, 7 to 9 minutes.

Using a folded kitchen towel to shield your fingers, steady an ear of corn stem end up at a 45-degree angle on a cutting board. With a sharp knife, cut downwards parallel to the ear to remove several rows of corn kernels. Turn the ear slightly and repeat until all the kernels have been removed from all the ears of corn. Transfer the kernels little by little to a serving bowl.

Sprinkle the corn kernels with the lime juice, chili powder, and salt, toss well, and serve immediately.

ginger butter corn

All-American corn on the cob gets an Asian twist.

4 servings

Preheat the grill.

Meanwhile, put the ears of corn in a microwave-proof dish, add 2 tablespoons of water, cover, and microwave just until the corn is tender, about 4 minutes. Drain the ears well, pat them dry with paper towels, and return them to the dish. In a small bowl, mash together the butter, ginger, and salt. Smear the butter mixture all over the corn. Set aside.

Carefully oil the grill rack. Place the corn on the grill and cook, turning frequently and basting with any butter remaining in the dish, until the corn kernels are flecked golden brown, 6 to 7 minutes. Serve immediately.

4 **ears fresh sweet corn, husks and silks removed**

3 **tablespoons unsalted butter, softened**

1 **tablespoon grated fresh ginger root**

¼ **teaspoon salt**

quick tips & variations

* Many markets today offer ready-to-cook ears of corn that have already had their husks and silk removed.
* If you like, substitute a dash of soy sauce for the salt.

vegetables

143

chili-dusted potato slices

These go great with boldly flavored red meat, poultry, or seafood dishes.

——— 4 servings ———

4 medium-sized baking potatoes, scrubbed but not peeled (about 2 pounds total weight)

½ cup extra-virgin olive oil

1 tablespoon mild to medium-hot pure chili powder

2 teaspoons dried oregano

1 teaspoon salt

Preheat the grill.

Meanwhile, cut the potatoes lengthwise into slices about ½ inch thick. Put the slices in a saucepan, add cold water to cover, season lightly with salt, cover, and bring to a boil. Uncover and continue boiling until the potatoes are tender enough to be pierced with the tip of a small, sharp knife, about 5 minutes. Drain well, rinse with cold running water until cool enough to handle, and then drain again. Pat the slices dry with paper towels.

Pour the olive oil onto a rimmed baking sheet large enough to hold all the potato slices side by side. Add the potatoes and turn them in the oil to coat them evenly on both sides. Just before grilling, sprinkle the potato slices evenly on both sides with the chili powder and the salt.

Carefully oil the grill rack. Place the potato slices on the grill and cook, turning once until they are golden brown and crisp, and basting them a few times with the remaining olive oil and seasonings in the dish, 12 to 14 minutes total cooking time.

quicktips &variations

* If your grill rack is widely spaced, or if the potatoes are on the long, narrow side, consider cutting them into slices at an angle.
* Substitute chili powder, the traditional Southwestern seasoning blend usually spiked with cumin and other spices, in place of the pure chili powder.
* For extra bright color and flavor, garnish the potato slices with chopped cilantro, chives, or Italian parsley after they come off the grill.

tuscan-style new potatoes with rosemary and sea salt

This recipe re-creates in a grill version the aromatic oven-roasted potatoes my wife, Katie, and I enjoyed on our honeymoon in Florence, Italy. Serve them with any kind of grilled meat or poultry.

— 4 servings

Preheat the grill. If using wooden or bamboo skewers, put them in a bowl of cold water to soak.

Meanwhile, put the potatoes in a saucepan, add cold water to cover, season lightly with salt, cover, and bring to a boil. Uncover and continue boiling until the potatoes are tender enough to be pierced with the tip of a small, sharp knife, 7 to 10 minutes. Drain well, rinse with cold running water until cool enough to handle, and then drain again and pat dry with a kitchen towel or paper towels. Pour the olive oil into a mixing bowl, add the potatoes, and turn them in the oil to coat them evenly. Just before grilling, combine the rosemary and salt in a small bowl and turn the potatoes in the mixture one by one to coat them before threading them onto skewers. Reserve the olive oil left in the bowl.

Carefully oil the grill rack. Place the potato skewers on the grill and cook, turning several times until they are uniformly golden brown and crisp, and basting them carefully a few times with the remaining olive oil, 16 to 18 minutes total cooking time.

2 pounds small new potatoes, 1 to 1½ inches in diameter (about 2 dozen total), washed and patted dry

¼ cup extra-virgin olive oil

3 tablespoons chopped fresh rosemary leaves

1½ tablespoons coarse sea salt or kosher salt

quick tips & variations

* Thin skewers work best for spearing the potatoes; larger ones run the risk of splitting the potatoes in half. Alternatively, you could grill the unskewered potatoes directly on a special grilling screen placed atop the grill rack to prevent them from falling through.
* If new potatoes are unavailable, substitute larger potatoes cut into wedges or slices as described in the recipes on pages 144 and 147.
* For an especially attractive and aromatic version of this recipe, seek out sturdy branches of rosemary. Strip them of all but a tuft of their leaves at one end and cut the other end to a point with a sharp knife to transform them into skewers for the potatoes.

vegetables

garlic-and-parsley
potato slices

When the grill menu is especially robust, featuring red meat, these golden-brown, aromatic potatoes make an ideal side dish.

———————— 4 to 6 servings ———

4 medium-sized baking potatoes, scrubbed but not peeled (about 3 pounds total weight)

6 tablespoons unsalted butter, melted

6 tablespoons extra-virgin olive oil

4 garlic cloves, peeled

1 teaspoon salt

4 tablespoons finely chopped fresh Italian parsley

quicktips
&variations

* Classic Idaho-type baking potatoes have just the right size and texture to work perfectly for this dish.
* For fewer losses, place the potato slices lengthwise at right angles to the bars of the grill rack.
* Be prepared for the fact that the potato skins may stick or become tattered during grilling. This just adds to the recipe's rustic nature.
* Add basil, chives, or other fresh herbs you like to the parsley scattered over the potatoes before serving.

Preheat the grill for medium-hot cooking.

Meanwhile, cut the potatoes lengthwise into slices about ½ inch thick. Put the slices in a saucepan, add cold water to cover, season lightly with salt, cover, and bring to a boil. Uncover and continue boiling until the potatoes are tender enough to be pierced with the tip of a small, sharp knife, about 5 minutes. Drain well, rinse with cold running water until cool enough to handle, and then drain again on paper towels.

Pour the melted butter and olive oil onto one or more rimmed baking sheets large enough to hold all the potato slices in a single layer. Press the garlic cloves through a garlic press and into the butter-oil mixture, then stir to blend. Add the potatoes and turn them in the garlic butter-oil to coat them evenly on both sides. Just before grilling, sprinkle the potato slices evenly on both sides with the salt.

Carefully oil the grill rack. Place the potato slices on the grill and cook, turning once, until they are golden brown and crisp, 12 to 15 minutes total. Remove from the grill to a serving dish and scatter the parsley on top.

sweet-hot sweet potato wedges

Serve these simple yet spectacular glazed sweet potatoes
with grilled poultry, lamb, or pork.

4 servings

Preheat the grill.

Meanwhile, prepare the sweet potatoes. Peel them, cut
them in half crosswise, then cut each half lengthwise into
6 equal wedges. Put the wedges in a saucepan, add cold
water to cover, season lightly with salt, cover, and bring to
a boil. Uncover, reduce the heat, and simmer gently until
the sweet potatoes are barely tender enough to be
pierced with the tip of a small, sharp knife, about 5 minutes. Drain well, rinse with cold running water until cool
enough to handle, and then drain again. Pat the wedges
dry and put them in a shallow dish.

Put the butter and marmalade in a small microwave-proof
bowl and heat in the microwave briefly, just until the butter melts. Add the chili powder and stir until blended.
Pour about two-thirds of the mixture over the sweet
potato wedges and turn them in it until evenly coated.
Just before grilling, sprinkle the wedges with salt and
black pepper to taste.

Carefully oil the grill rack. Place the sweet potato wedges
on the grill and cook, turning them 2 or 3 times until they
are tender and are just beginning to char at their edges,
about 10 minutes total. Just before the wedges are done,
use a long-handled spoon or brush to baste and glaze
them with the remaining butter-marmalade mixture.

2 large sweet potatoes (about
2 pounds total weight)

4 tablespoons unsalted butter,
melted

4 tablespoons fine-cut orange
marmalade

$1/4$ to $1/2$ teaspoon medium-hot
pure chili powder

Salt

Black pepper

quick tips
& variations

* If you like sweet potato peels, save time
by leaving the potatoes unpeeled. But
take care to cut out any blemishes.
* The sweet potatoes may also be cut crosswise or diagonally into $2/3$- to $3/4$-inch-
thick slices.

marshmallow-topped maple-glazed sweet potatoes

This grill version of a popular holiday side dish goes very well with simply grilled turkey cutlets or chicken.

4 servings

2 large sweet potatoes (about 2 pounds total weight)

4 tablespoons unsalted butter, melted

4 tablespoons pure maple syrup

½ teaspoon ground cinnamon

⅛ teaspoon ground nutmeg

1½ cups miniature marshmallows

quicktips
&variations

* A dry, long-handled spoon may be of assistance in placing marshmallows atop slices that are closer to the center of the grill without exposing your hands to too much heat.

Preheat the grill.

Meanwhile, peel the sweet potatoes and trim off their pointy ends. Cut diagonally into slices ⅔ to ¾ inch thick. Put the slices in a saucepan, add cold water to cover, season lightly with salt, cover, and bring to a boil. Uncover, reduce the heat, and simmer gently until the sweet potatoes are barely tender enough to be pierced with the tip of a small, sharp knife, about 5 minutes. Drain well, rinse with cold running water until cool enough to handle, and then drain again. Pat the slices dry and put them in a shallow dish.

Put the butter and maple syrup in a small microwave-proof bowl and heat in the microwave briefly, just until the butter melts. Add the cinnamon and nutmeg and stir until blended. Lightly brush the sweet potato slices on both sides with the mixture, setting the remainder of it aside.

Carefully oil the grill rack. Place the sweet potato slices on the grill and cook, basting them with half of the remaining butter-syrup mixture, until their undersides are nicely browned, 6 to 7 minutes. Turn them over, baste with the remaining mixture, and carefully top with the marshmallows, distributing them evenly among the slices. Continue cooking until the marshmallows have melted, the undersides are golden, and the sweet potatoes are tender when gently prodded with a fork, 6 to 7 minutes more.

cardamom-ginger carrots

Just a hint of exotic spices adds special character to simply grilled carrots, a great companion for grilled meat or poultry.

—— 4 servings ——

1 pound carrots of even 1-inch diameter

1 tablespoon unsalted butter, melted

1 tablespoon extra-virgin olive oil

¼ teaspoon ground cardamom

¼ teaspoon ground ginger

¼ teaspoon salt

¼ teaspoon sugar

2 tablespoons finely chopped fresh Italian parsley

Preheat the grill.

Meanwhile, prepare the carrots. Scrub them under cold running water and cut them into pieces 3 to 4 inches long. In a mixing bowl, stir together the butter, oil, cardamom, ginger, salt, and sugar. Add the carrot pieces and turn them in the mixture to coat them evenly.

Carefully oil the grill rack. Place the carrot pieces on the grill at right angles to its wires and cook, turning frequently and basting occasionally with the butter mixture left in the bowl, until the carrots are tender and golden brown, about 15 minutes. Transfer to a serving bowl and garnish with the parsley.

quick tips
& variations

* Many markets sell carrot varieties that are almost perfectly cylindrical in form rather than tapered. These will cook more evenly on the grill.
* There is no need to waste time peeling the carrots. A quick scrubbing is fine.
* You can substitute ground coriander for the cardamom. Chives or basil may be substituted for all or part of the parsley.

fennel bulb with lemon, olive oil, and parmesan shavings

One taste of this has the power to transport you to an Italian hillside in summer. The sweet, anise-scented fennel bulb is ideal for grilling and serving with lamb, beef, or poultry.

— 4 servings —

2 **fennel bulbs (about 1½ pounds total weight)**

4 **tablespoons extra-virgin olive oil**

4 **tablespoons lemon juice**

Salt

Black pepper

½-ounce block Parmesan cheese

Preheat the grill.

While the grill is heating, prepare the fennel. With a sharp knife, trim off any stalks, blemished outer layers, or tough root ends. Cut the bulbs in half lengthwise. Then place each half cut side down and cut it lengthwise into four wedges. Put the wedges in a mixing bowl and toss with the olive oil and lemon juice until thoroughly coated.

Carefully oil the grill rack. Season the fennel wedges to taste with salt and black pepper and put them on the grill. Cook, turning two or three times, until golden brown, 6 to 8 minutes total cooking time. Transfer the fennel to a serving plate. With a swivel-bladed vegetable peeler, cut the Parmesan into thin shavings over the fennel.

quicktips &variations

* After cutting the fennel bulbs in half, cut them vertically into ½-inch-thick slices.
* Instead of messing with the vegetable peeler, sprinkle the hot-off-the-grill fennel with grated Parmesan cheese.
* Serve the fennel hot or lukewarm as part of a grilled antipasto platter.

portobello mushrooms with garlic-parsley-basil butter

Fresh portobello mushroom caps are often compared to steaks, and they come out extremely well when seasoned and grilled in the same manner as meat.

— 4 servings —

Preheat the grill.

Meanwhile, prepare the mushrooms, brushing them clean with a damp cloth or paper towel and removing their stems. Press the garlic clove through a garlic press and into a small bowl. Add the butter, basil, and parsley, then stir to blend. Brush the mushrooms all over on both sides with the olive oil.

Carefully oil the grill rack. Season the mushrooms on both sides with salt and black pepper to taste, and place them stemmed side down on the grill. Cook 4 to 5 minutes. Turn the mushrooms over, spoon the seasoned butter evenly into their caps, and continue grilling until the mushrooms are tender, the butter has melted, and their undersides are golden brown, 4 to 5 minutes more.

4 large portobello mushrooms (about ¾ pound total weight)

1 or 2 garlic cloves, peeled

3 tablespoons unsalted butter, softened

1 tablespoon finely chopped fresh basil leaves

1 tablespoon finely chopped fresh Italian parsley

2 tablespoons extra-virgin olive oil

Salt

Black pepper

quick tips & variations

* Add other fresh herbs such as chives to the butter.
* Substitute finely minced shallots for the garlic.
* For a vegetarian main course, serve each grilled mushroom in a good-quality burger bun or soft bakery roll that you've split, brushed with a little olive oil, and toasted on the grill. Dijon mustard goes very well with these burgers.

vegetables

151

teriyaki
shiitake
mushrooms

Among the meatiest of mushrooms, fresh shiitakes take well to the seasonings commonly found in Japanese teriyaki sauce. Serve these as a side dish for Asian-style poultry, seafood, or meat dishes, or as a main dish over rice. They're also delicious in split, toasted burger buns.

———— 4 servings ————

8 large fresh shiitake mushrooms (about 1 pound total weight)

3 tablespoons soy sauce

1½ tablespoons rice vinegar

1 tablespoon sugar

1½ tablespoons corn oil or vegetable oil

2 scallions, thinly sliced

1 tablespoon toasted or black sesame seeds

Preheat the grill.

Meanwhile, prepare the mushrooms. With a small, sharp knife, cut off the stems flush with the caps, and discard the stems. With a damp paper towel, wipe the caps clean. In a mixing bowl, stir together the soy sauce, rice vinegar, and sugar until the sugar dissolves. Stir in the oil. Add the mushroom caps and turn them to coat them thoroughly, then leave them in the soy and vinegar mixture gills down.

Carefully oil the grill rack. Put the mushroom caps on the rack gill sides down. Cook until their undersides are golden, basting once or twice with a little of the soy mixture, about 5 minutes total. Turn the mushrooms over and continue grilling and basting with the remaining soy and vinegar mixture until the undersides are nicely browned, about 5 minutes more. Turn the caps over once more and grill about 1 minute more. Serve immediately, gill sides up, garnished with sliced scallions and sesame seeds.

quick tips
& variations

* This recipe works equally well with big portobello mushroom caps, and can be done with a similar weight of good-sized cultivated mushrooms.
* Add a dash of Asian hot chili-flavored sesame oil to the soy mixture if you like.

radicchio with balsamic vinegar and dijon mustard

Serve these grilled quarters of purple-and-white-striped radicchio with robust, Mediterranean-flavored grilled meat dishes. Or top them with Parmesan shavings and serve as an appetizer or as part of an antipasto platter.

— 4 servings

Preheat the grill.

Meanwhile, cut the radicchio lengthwise into quarters, leaving the leaves attached at each head's core. In a bowl, stir together the vinegar, mustard, salt, and black pepper. Stirring continuously, slowly pour in the olive oil. Add the radicchio quarters and turn them to coat them evenly with the dressing, leaving them resting cut sides down.

Carefully oil the grill rack. Place the radicchio quarters on the grill and cook, turning several times until they are golden brown and tender-crisp, and basting them a few times with the remaining dressing, 6 to 8 minutes total cooking time. Remove from the grill and, before serving, top them with Parmesan shavings if you like.

2 heads radicchio (10 to 12 ounces total weight)

1 tablespoon balsamic vinegar

1 teaspoon regular Dijon mustard

¼ teaspoon salt

¼ teaspoon black pepper

3 tablespoons extra-virgin olive oil

1 ounce block Parmesan cheese, thinly shaved with a vegetable peeler (optional)

quick tips & variations

* Buy a good-quality, aged balsamic vinegar imported from Modena, Italy. It will have a good, complex flavor and syrupy consistency to complement the bitterness of the radicchio.
* Heads of Belgian endive, cut lengthwise in half, may be substituted for the radicchio.

broccoli flowers
with lemon-dijon
vinaigrette

A simple salad dressing serves as both marinade and sauce for big florets of broccoli quickly browned on the grill.

———— 4 servings ——

¾ **pound large fresh broccoli florets**

¼ **cup lemon juice**

1½ **tablespoons Dijon mustard, preferably coarse-grained "country style"**

1 **teaspoon sugar**

½ **teaspoon salt**

¼ **teaspoon black pepper**

½ **cup extra-virgin olive oil**

Preheat the grill.

Meanwhile, put the broccoli florets in a microwave-safe container, add a tablespoon or two of water, cover, and microwave on high until tender-crisp, 1 to 2 minutes. Remove the broccoli from the microwave and drain, taking care to avoid direct exposure to any steam from the container. In a mixing bowl, stir together the lemon juice, mustard, sugar, salt, and black pepper. Whisking continuously with a fork or a small wire whisk, slowly drizzle in the olive oil. Add the broccoli to this dressing and turn once to coat it thoroughly, leaving the florets stem ends up in the mixture.

Carefully oil the grill rack. Remove the broccoli from the bowl and shake off any excess dressing, letting it fall back into the bowl. Set the bowl aside. Place the broccoli on the grill and cook, turning occasionally, until golden brown, about 4 minutes. Return the grilled broccoli to the dressing and turn once to coat it. Serve hot, warm, or at room temperature.

quicktips
&variations

* Many markets and greengrocers today sell broccoli in precisely the form that works best for this recipe—big flower heads that have been cut leaving just an inch or so of stem. These make an impressive presentation and can be grilled just as they are, without falling through the grill rack.
* If you can't find broccoli in this form, buy a larger quantity of whole broccoli and cut off the large floret ends yourself. The stems may be peeled and grilled on their own, lightly coated with olive oil and seasoned with salt and pepper.
* Try preparing cauliflower in the same way.
* Serve the broccoli with grilled steaks, poultry, or seafood.

broccolini
with garlic
and oil

Markets today are starting to carry bunches of this slender, mild-tasting cousin to broccoli, which grills quickly and makes a great accompaniment for meat or an addition to a mixed-grill vegetable antipasto.

——— 4 servings ———

Preheat the grill.

Meanwhile, prepare the broccolini. Trim off any tough stalk ends. Press the garlic clove through a garlic press and into a shallow dish. Stir in the olive oil. Add the broccolini and turn once to coat them with the garlic and oil.

Carefully oil the grill rack. Season the broccolini with salt and black pepper to taste, and spread the stalks evenly on the grill at right angles to the rack's wires. Cook, turning occasionally, until tender and lightly browned, 7 to 8 minutes.

¾ pound broccolini

1 garlic clove, peeled

2 tablespoons extra-virgin olive oil

Salt

Black pepper

quick tips & variations

* Broccolini is sometimes labeled "baby broccoli" in supermarkets. It is also sold under the brand name Asparation, presumably a play on its resemblance in size, and slightly in flavor, to asparagus.
* Slender stalks of asparagus may be substituted.
* Finely chopped hard-boiled egg makes a lovely, classic garnish.
* Offer lemon wedges, if you like, for guests to add a squeeze to each serving.

garlicky baby squash skewers

Immature little summer squashes of various kinds have become so popular that many markets now offer them regularly. They cook quickly on the grill and, on or off the skewers on which they cook, make a lovely little side dish for meat, poultry, or seafood.

— 4 servings —

1 pound assorted baby summer squashes such as yellow or green pattypan or yellow or green zucchini

1½ tablespoons extra-virgin olive oil

1 clove garlic, peeled

Salt

Black pepper

Preheat the grill. If using wooden or bamboo skewers, soak them in cold water.

Meanwhile, trim any tough stems or blemished flower ends from the squashes. Put the olive oil in a large bowl. Squeeze the garlic clove through a garlic press and into the bowl, then stir the oil and garlic together. Add the squashes and turn them in the oil to coat them evenly. Thread the squashes onto skewers.

Just before grilling, sprinkle the squashes with salt and black pepper to taste. Carefully oil the grill rack. Grill the squashes until tender and golden brown, turning the skewers once or twice and making sure the squashes turn with them, 10 to 12 minutes total.

quick tips & variations

* If baby squashes are unavailable, use the smallest green or yellow zucchini you can find, cutting them into 1-inch chunks and skewering each chunk through its colored sides.
* Add a little spice of your choice, sprinkling on some mild pure chili powder or some ground coriander along with the salt and pepper.
* Use more slender skewers to help prevent the squashes from splitting when speared.

curry-dusted
acorn squash
crescents

The sweet, earthy flavor and golden color of acorn squash go beautifully with mild curry powder to make an ideal companion to plain or spicy grilled meat or poultry.

———— 4 servings ————

1   whole acorn squash, about 1¼ pounds

2   tablespoons unsalted butter, melted

2   teaspoons mild curry powder

1   teaspoon sugar

    Salt

    Black pepper

Preheat the grill.

Meanwhile, prepare the squash. With a large, sharp knife, carefully cut the squash in half through its stem and bottom ends. Trim off the stem and bottom and, with a sharp-edged spoon, scoop out and discard the seeds. Place each half cut side down and cut it crosswise into semicircles about ½ inch thick. Put the squash crescents in a saucepan of lightly salted water. Put the pan over medium-high heat, cover, and bring to a boil, then lower the heat and simmer just until the squash crescents are barely tender when a sharp knife tip is inserted, about 5 minutes. Drain, rinse with cold running water to cool the squash down, then drain the crescents well and pat them dry with paper towels.

Pour the melted butter into a baking dish large enough to hold the squash crescents in a single layer. Add the squash crescents and turn them in the butter to coat them evenly. Sprinkle them on both sides with the curry powder, sugar, salt, and black pepper to taste.

Carefully oil the grill rack. Place the squash crescents at right angles to the rack's wires and cook until golden brown, carefully turning once with a spatula, 10 to 12 minutes total. Remove to a platter and serve immediately.

quicktips &variations

*   The shape and size of acorn squash works particularly well for this recipe. Feel free to substitute a similar quantity of another winter squash, cut into slices of the same thickness.
*   Curry powder quickly diminishes in aromatic power. Buy a good-quality imported blend, in small quantities, from an Indian market or another source that has a good turnover of product.
*   Either of the yogurt-based raita sauces in the recipes on pages 80 and 105 go very well with the squash, whether or not it is served as a side dish with those recipes.

vegetables

endive with olive oil and sea salt

Some people are indifferent to endive, finding it bland at best and slightly bitter at worst. Brief grilling brings out a richer flavor in the vegetable, without diminishing its refreshing crispness. Serve with fish, poultry, or meat.

— 4 servings —

4 heads Belgian endive, cut in halves lengthwise

2 tablespoons extra-virgin olive oil

1 teaspoon sea salt

Preheat the grill.

Meanwhile, put the endive halves in a shallow dish and rub them evenly with the olive oil. Sprinkle evenly with the sea salt.

Carefully oil the grill rack. Grill the endive halves until heated through and lightly golden brown, turning once, 4 to 5 minutes total. Serve hot or lukewarm.

quick tips & variations

* Try adding a dab of Dijon mustard to the oil before rubbing it on the endive halves.
* Top the grilled endive with Parmesan shavings, as in Fennel Bulb with Lemon, Olive Oil, and Parmesan Shavings, page 150.
* Offer the endive as part of a grilled antipasto platter.

brussels sprouts
with grainy mustard

An antidote to Brussels sprouts in their tired, old, boiled guise, this recipe produces a vegetable with a golden-brown surface that shows off its texture and flavor to surprisingly good advantage.

— 4 servings —

Preheat the grill. If using wooden or bamboo skewers, put them in a bowl of cold water to soak.

Meanwhile, prepare the Brussels sprouts. Trim their tough stem ends and remove any tough or blemished outer leaves. Put them in a microwave-proof bowl with a tablespoon or so of cold water, cover with plastic wrap, and cook in the microwave on the High setting until tender-crisp, 2 to 3 minutes. In a small bowl, stir together the olive oil and mustard. Drain the Brussels sprouts and pat them dry with paper towels. Return them to the bowl, add the mustard-oil mixture, and toss well to coat the sprouts. Leave them until they are cool enough to handle, then thread them onto skewers, reserving the oil and mustard left in the bowl.

Carefully oil the grill rack. Sprinkle the sprouts with salt. Place the skewers on the grill, baste immediately with the remaining mustard-oil mixture, and cook, turning two or three times, until the Brussels sprouts are lightly browned all over, 4 to 6 minutes total.

¾ **pound medium-sized Brussels sprouts**

2 **tablespoons extra-virgin olive oil**

1 **tablespoon grainy Dijon mustard**

¼ **teaspoon salt**

quick tips & variations

* If the Brussels sprouts you buy are too small, they may split when you try to skewer them. If that is the case, cook them on a smaller-mesh cooking grid placed atop the grill rack.

vegetables

teriyaki
tofu

Tofu, or soybean curd, cooks surprisingly well on the grill as a vegetarian main course or as a side dish, gaining rich flavor and a slightly chewy texture. The trick is to use extra-firm tofu and to drain it well.

—— 4 servings ——

1 package extra-firm tofu, drained (about 15 ounces)

¼ cup soy sauce

¼ cup rice vinegar

2 teaspoons sugar

1 clove garlic, peeled

1-inch piece fresh ginger, peeled and cut into 4 pieces

2 tablespoons toasted Asian sesame oil

2 scallions, trimmed and very thinly sliced

1 tablespoon toasted or black Japanese sesame seeds

Preheat the grill.

Meanwhile, line two large plates with a triple thickness of paper towels. Cut the drained block of tofu horizontally into four equal slices and place two side by side on each plate. Cover each plate of tofu with another triple thickness of paper towels, then top it with another plate and weight it down with heavy cans to help press excess moisture out of the tofu. Leave for about 15 minutes.

Meanwhile, in a shallow baking dish large enough to hold the tofu slices in a single layer, make the teriyaki mixture. Pour in the soy sauce, vinegar, and sugar. Using a garlic press, press the garlic and then the ginger pieces into the dish. Stir well, until the sugar has mostly dissolved. Stir in the sesame oil. As soon as the tofu is drained, carefully transfer the tofu slices to the teriyaki mixture, turning them to coat, and leave them to marinate for about 15 minutes, turning them once again.

Carefully oil the grill rack. Gently place the tofu slices on the grill and cook, turning once, until they are golden brown, basting them a few times with the teriyaki marinade left in the baking dish, 5 to 6 minutes total cooking time. Remove the tofu slices from the grill and, before serving, top them the with scallions and sesame seeds.

quicktips
&variations

* Feel free to substitute about ¹/₂ cup of good-quality commercial, bottled teriyaki sauce for the mixture in this recipe.
* For a vegetarian grilled sandwich, serve a tofu slice on a grill-toasted whole-wheat burger bun or roll. Add some sprouts or shredded carrots if you like.
* If your grill rack's bars are widely spread or very thin, consider cooking the tofu on smaller-mesh cooking grid placed atop the grill rack.

fire-licked guacamole

Roasting the chilies, tomatoes, and onion for this variation on the classic avocado dip gives it a rich, slightly
smoky flavor. Serve it as you would a salsa to accompany
well-spiced main courses, or offer it with chips while a
longer-cooking main dish continues to grill.

—— 4 to 6 servings ——

2 red or green jalapeño chilies

2 ripe but firm Roma tomatoes

1 small yellow onion

2 ripe Hass avocados

1 lime or lemon, cut in half

2 tablespoons finely chopped
   fresh cilantro

   Salt

Preheat the grill.

Carefully oil the grill rack. Place the chilies, tomatoes, and
onion on the grill and cook, turning occasionally with
long-handled metal tongs, until their skins are evenly
blistered and blackened, 10 to 12 minutes. Remove them
from the heat to a heatproof plate, cover them tightly
with aluminum foil, and leave until cool enough to handle,
about 10 minutes.

With your fingertips and a small, sharp knife, peel away
the blackened skins from the vegetables. Carefully slit
open the chilies and remove and discard their stems,
seeds, and veins. Mince the chilies and put in a mixing
bowl. Cut the tomatoes in half, use the handle of a teaspoon to scoop out and discard their seeds, then cut their
flesh into ½-inch dice and add to the bowl. Cut the onion
into ½-inch cubes and add to the bowl.

Halve and pit the avocados. With a tablespoon, scoop out
their flesh and add to the mixing bowl. Squeeze the lime
or lemon halves into the bowl, using the outstretched
fingers of one hand to strain out any seeds. With a fork,
coarsely mash the avocados and mix them with the other
ingredients. Add the cilantro and season with salt to taste.

quicktips &variations

* If you're averse to even a hint of strong
  spices, substitute a milder-tasting long
  green chili, known variously as an Anaheim
  or New Mexican.
* When working with any chilies, take care
  not to touch your eyes or any other sensi-
  tive areas, because the peppers' volatile
  oils can cause painful burning sensations.
  Wear gloves if you're particularly sensi-
  tive. At the very least, wash your hands
  thoroughly with warm, soapy water after
  stemming, peeling, and seeding the
  chilies.

vegetables

161

fire-roasted chili-tomato salsa

So many of the best Mexican salsas get some of their seasoning from a lick of live fire. Here's a good, all-purpose version that you can get started on the grill before you cook the meat, poultry, or seafood you plan to serve it with.

———— 4 to 6 servings ——

¾ pound firm, ripe Roma tomatoes, cored, halved, and seeded

2 fresh green pasilla or jalapeño chilies

2 tablespoons extra-virgin olive oil

2 tablespoons finely chopped fresh cilantro

1 tablespoon lime juice

½ teaspoon salt

quicktips & variations

* Use your choice of mild, medium-hot, or spicy fresh chilies.
* If you like, add three or four grilled Cantina Scallions (page 140), chopping them up with the other vegetables.
* The salsa is also good cold. Refrigerate it in a covered container after it has cooled to lukewarm. Before using, taste and add a little more salt, as chilling salsa will mute the flavors.

Preheat the grill.

When the grill is ready, carefully oil the grill rack. Brush the tomatoes and chilies with 1 tablespoon of the olive oil and put them on the grill. Cook, turning the tomatoes once and the peppers several times, until the vegetables are evenly browned and tender, about 6 minutes total for the tomatoes and 10 minutes for the chilies. As they are done, remove them to a bowl and cover with aluminum foil.

When the chilies are cool enough to handle, peel off and discard their blistered skins. Then, with a small, sharp knife, slit open the chilies and remove their stems, seeds, and white veins.

With a sharp knife or in a food processor with the metal blade, finely chop together the tomatoes, chilies, and cilantro. Mix in the lime juice, remaining olive oil, and salt. Serve warm.

fruit & other desserts

Mention the concept of a grilled dessert, and the only thought that instantly enters the minds of most people is s'mores. That campfire favorite is made by toasting (or, more often, carbonizing) a marshmallow on the end of a long fork or stick held over the dying coals, then quickly clamping it with a square of chocolate between two graham crackers.

Counter that concept with the idea of grilling fruit, and you're likely to get a puzzled look in return. Yet many different kinds of fruit cook beautifully over a grill. This is especially true when the coals are dying (or the gas dial has been turned down) and the gentle heat warms the fruit through, slowly caramelizing its natural sugars, slightly softening its texture, and contributing an appealing golden color.

All but one of the fruit recipes that follow make excellent desserts at the end of a grilled meal. (The exception is Bacon-Wrapped Brandied Dried Plums, page 166, which for obvious reasons is better suited as an appetizer.) Many also double well as side dishes for main courses, particularly those featuring pork, that benefit from the contrast of fruity flavor.

In addition, I've included two end-of-the-meal recipes based on flour tortillas, including S'Mores "Quesadillas," a unique approach to making s'mores (page 171). Like the fruit recipes, these will cook best, with no trace of conflicting flavors, if you take care to scrub the grill rack thoroughly with a wire brush and then oil it with a flavorless oil, such as canola or corn, just before cooking.

pie-spiced apple rings with butter and brown sugar

Serve these in smaller portions as an accompaniment to grilled pork. Or accompany larger portions with vanilla ice cream for dessert.

———— 4 servings ————

2 large tart-sweet cooking apples such as Granny Smith, Jonathan, or Pippin

2 tablespoons unsalted butter, melted

1 teaspoon ground cinnamon

Pinch of ground nutmeg

¼ cup light brown sugar

quick tips & variations

* Tart, crisp cooking apples such as Granny Smith will yield the best flavor and texture.
* Scoring the apples before you core and slice them will stop the skin from puckering on the grill and thus maintain the shape of the rings.
* If you already have it in your cupboard, substitute a commercial apple pie spice blend for the spices given in the recipe.

Preheat the grill.

Meanwhile, prepare the apples. With a small, sharp knife, lightly slit the skin of the apples vertically from stem to flower end about six times, evenly spaced. With an apple corer, remove the cores. Cut the apples crosswise into rings about ¾ inch thick. In a small bowl, stir together the butter, cinnamon, and nutmeg. Spread the sugar on a small plate. Just before cooking, lightly brush the apple rings on both sides with the butter-spice mixture. Then press each ring on both sides into the sugar to coat it, placing the coated rings side by side on a large plate or platter.

Carefully oil the grill rack. Place the apple rings on the grill rack and cook them until they are golden and tender-crisp, turning them once halfway through, about 8 minutes total cooking time.

cheese-stuffed pears

Tangy cheeses always go well with pears at the end of a meal. These cook especially well over a dying fire.

4 servings

2 firm but ripe eating pears, such as Bartlett or Comice

2 tablespoons lemon juice

3 ounces soft, blue-veined cheese such as Gorgonzola, Stilton, or Roquefort

4 tablespoons honey

Preheat the grill.

Meanwhile, prepare the pears and the cheese mixture. Cut each pear lengthwise in half. With a sharp-edged teaspoon, scoop out the core of each half, forming a nicely shaped hollow into which the cheese will go. Put the pear halves in a dish large enough to hold them side by side. Rub them all over with the lemon juice, then leave them cut sides down in the juice. Put the cheese in a small mixing bowl and add 2 tablespoons of the honey. Use a fork to mash together the cheese and honey. Set aside.

Just before cooking, smear the pears all over with the remaining honey. Carefully oil the grill rack. Put the pear halves on the grill cut sides down and cook until they are lightly browned, 2 to 3 minutes. With tongs, carefully turn the pear halves over. Immediately spoon the cheese-honey mixture into their hollows. Cover the grill and cook until the cheese begins to melt, 3 to 4 minutes more. Serve immediately.

quick tips & variations

* A soft, creamy variety of feta cheese may be used in place of the blue cheese.
* If you like, add one heaping tablespoon of toasted chopped hazelnuts, walnuts, or pecans to the cheese-honey mixture. Whole pine nuts are another good choice.
* If fresh mint is available, finely chop a few leaves and add them to the lemon juice you use to coat the cut pears. Use a small sprig of mint as a garnish for each serving.

bacon-wrapped brandied dried plums

Just three simple ingredients here yield a surprisingly sophisticated taste. Serve these plums as an appetizer or as an accompaniment to grilled pork main courses.

— 4 servings —

12 large, plump, pitted dried plums (prunes)

3 tablespoons brandy or cognac

6 slices bacon, cut crosswise in halves

Preheat the grill. If using wooden or bamboo skewers, put them in a bowl of cold water to soak.

Meanwhile, prepare the dried plums. Put them in a small mixing bowl. In a small saucepan, warm the brandy over medium heat for about 1 minute (be careful, as brandy is flammable). Pour the warm brandy over the dried plums and leave them to soak for about 10 minutes, turning them once or twice. Then, one at a time, roll up each dried plum in one of the bacon slice halves and thread it onto a skewer, passing the skewer carefully through the overlapping ends of the bacon strip, the dried plum, and the bacon on the other side.

Carefully oil the grill rack. Place the skewers on the grill rack and cook, turning once, until the bacon is crisply browned, 8 to 10 minutes total.

quicktips &variations

* Pitted dried plums (prunes) are also sold today flavored with natural orange or lemon essence. These are an excellent choice for the recipe. Or just add 1 table-spoon of grated orange zest or lemon zest to the brandy and dried plums during soaking.
* Substitute strips of thinly sliced pro-sciutto or smoked ham for the bacon.
* For an extra-rich version, stuff a $1/2$-inch cube of mild cheese such as Monterey Jack or mozzarella into each dried plum before you wrap it in the bacon.
* If the wires on your grill rack are spaced closely enough, you can dispense with skewers. Instead, soak large wooden cocktail picks, one for each dried plum, in water while the dried plums are steeping in the brandy. Then, use a cocktail pick to secure each individual morsel. Be sure to alert your guests to remove the picks before eating the dried plums.

chocolate-stuffed honeyed figs

Figs and chocolate make a seductive combination, especially when they're warmed together over a dying fire at the end of a grilled meal. Use fresh figs when they're in season, and dried ones at other times of year.

4 servings

Preheat the grill. If using wooden or bamboo skewers, put them in a bowl of cold water to soak.

Meanwhile, prepare the figs. With the tip of a small, sharp knife, cut a small slit from one side of the fig into its center. With a fingertip, push about ½ teaspoon of chocolate chips deep into the pocket. Thread the figs onto skewers, passing the skewer slightly off-center through the slit side to help secure the chocolate inside, and keeping the skewered figs slit sides up.

Carefully oil the grill rack. Drizzle the honey over the slit sides of the figs. Place the skewered figs on the grill, slit sides up, and cook, covered, just until they are heated and their undersides have turned golden brown, 2 to 3 minutes. Serve immediately.

1 dozen small, fresh or large, dried whole figs

2 tablespoons semisweet or milk chocolate chips

2 tablespoons honey

quick tips & variations

* When working with dried figs, you may have to manipulate them slightly before cutting the slits, pulling the stem of each fig outward to maneuver the fruit back into its original form. Once that is done, a dried fig is quite easy to slit, and you'll find a natural little pocket inside it ready for stuffing.
* The hot stuffed figs are also excellent served over a scoop of your favorite ice cream and drizzled with chocolate sauce or more honey.

bananas with brown sugar sesame butter

A treat for banana fans, this quick dessert is simple as can be. The optional sesame oil contributes a stronger sesame flavor if you'd like one.

— 4 servings —

4 ripe but firm bananas, peels left on

2 tablespoons unsalted butter, softened

2 tablespoons dark brown sugar

2 teaspoons toasted or black sesame seeds

1 teaspoon Asian toasted sesame oil (optional)

Pinch of salt

quicktips &variations

* For perfectly ripened bananas, look for those whose yellow skins have no traces of green but are lightly speckled with brown or black spots. If no such fruit are available, buy unripened bananas and let them ripen at room temperature for up to several days.
* For an elegant elaboration of this recipe, remove the grilled bananas from the heat and, with a spoon, scoop the chunks and their sauce directly from the peels and onto scoops of good-quality vanilla ice cream or frozen yogurt.

Preheat the grill.

With a sharp knife, cut each banana symmetrically lengthwise in half. Leaving each banana half nestled inside its peel, and without cutting the peel at all, with the knife tip cut each banana half crosswise into bite-sized chunks. Place the banana halves skin sides down on a large platter.

In a bowl, use a fork to mash together the butter, brown sugar, sesame seeds, sesame oil (if desired), and salt. Spread the mixture evenly over the cut sides of each banana half, keeping it within the border of the peel.

Carefully oil the grill rack. Place the banana halves skins down on the grill rack, cover the grill, and cook until the skins are evenly blackened and the butter topping is bubbly, about 4 minutes. Transfer the banana halves to individual serving plates and serve immediately.

brown sugar–crusted pineapple rings

An outstanding, simple grilled dessert, this also makes an excellent counterpoint to such spicy dishes as Jamaican-Style Jerked Pork Tenderloin (page 72).

———— 4 to 8 servings ————

Preheat the grill.

When the fire is ready, brush the pineapple rings on both sides with the melted butter. Sprinkle the brown sugar on a plate and turn the rings in the sugar to coat them on both sides, gently but firmly pressing the sugar into the pineapple with your fingertips.

Carefully oil the grill rack. Place the pineapple rings on the grill and cook until lightly browned, 2 to 3 minutes per side. Remove the rings from the heat to a serving dish. Serve hot or lukewarm.

1½ **pounds peeled and cored fresh pineapple, cut crosswise into 8 rings**

3 **tablespoons unsalted butter, melted**

6 **tablespoons light or dark brown sugar**

quick tips & variations

* For convenience, look in your supermarket produce section for packages of already peeled and cored whole fresh pineapple, ready for you to slice into rings.
* To counterpoint spicy main courses, the flavor of pineapple comes across especially well when the fruit is served lukewarm. So put it on the grill at the same time as the recipe it's accompanying, then remove the pineapple and let it stand at room temperature while the main course finishes cooking.
* The pineapple rings are also spectacular served atop scoops of vanilla ice cream or tropical sorbet to end a grilled meal. In that case, you may have to add a few minutes of cooking time if the fire begins to wane.

fruit & other desserts

169

cinnamon sugar tortillas

You won't believe how delicious this understated little recipe can be, producing results akin to a crisp cinnamon pastry. It cooks up especially well at the end of a grilled meal, when the fire is a bit past its peak of hotness.

—— 4 servings ——

4 tablespoons unsalted butter, softened

1½ tablespoons sugar

1½ teaspoons ground cinnamon

4 large flour tortillas

Preheat the grill.

Meanwhile, in a small bowl, use a fork to mash together the butter, sugar, and cinnamon. With a table knife, spread the mixture evenly on one side of each tortilla. Then fold each tortilla in half, with the butter mixture inside.

Carefully oil the grill rack. Put the folded tortillas on the grill and cook until deep golden brown and crisp, turning once or twice, 3 to 5 minutes in all, depending on the fire's heat. Remove the tortillas from the heat to a cutting board and cut each one into four to six wedges.

quick tips & variations

* This recipe gives delicious, wholesome-tasting results when made with whole-wheat tortillas.
* For an impressive, indulgent dessert, array the wedges of each tortilla around a scoop of good-quality ice cream. The favorite flavor in my house for this combination is "dulce de leche," flavored and swirled with the sweet, brown caramelized milk popular in Latin cultures. It is now widely available.
* If you want to embellish the tortillas even a step further, scatter a few chocolate chips over the butter before folding the tortillas.

s'mores "quesadillas"

Sure, burn your marshmallows or your fingers over the grill if you like! This recipe takes advantage of the neutral taste of flour tortillas, transforming them into an unusual vehicle for the old campfire favorite. Although I respectfully dispute his judgment on this, my son, Jake, insists that the recipe works even better if you double the quantities of all ingredients for the filling.

— 4 servings —

Preheat the grill.

Meanwhile, in a small bowl, use a fork to mash together the butter and sugar. Lightly spread the butter-sugar mixture on one side of each tortilla. On half of the buttered side, evenly sprinkle the chocolate chips, leaving a ¼- to ½-inch margin along the curved edge. Then, with your hands, crumble the graham crackers over the chocolate. Finally, scatter the marshmallows on top and fold the tortilla in half to enclose the filling.

Carefully oil the grill rack. Put the folded tortillas on the grill and cook until deep golden brown and crisp, carefully turning once by lifting the curved edges and flipping them gently, 3 to 5 minutes cooking time, depending on the fire's heat. Remove the tortillas from the heat to a cutting board and cut each one into four to six wedges.

2 tablespoons unsalted butter, softened

1 teaspoon sugar

4 large flour tortillas

1¼ cups semisweet or milk chocolate chocolate chips

4 whole individual rectangular sheets graham crackers

1¼ cups miniature marshmallows

quicktips &variations

* Experiment with flavored graham crackers or with the white chocolate or butterscotch-flavored chips now sold in supermarket baking sections.
* Serve the s'mores wedges with your favorite ice cream.

index